BASEBALL:

DIAMOND IN THE ROUGH

IRVING A. LEITNER

CRITERION BOOKS

NEW YORK · LONDON

This book is dedicated with love
to my two sons,
Peter and Richard,
and to all boys everywhere.

ACKNOWLEDGMENTS

I wish to express my thanks and gratitude to the New York Public Library for use of the Frederick Lewis Allen Memorial Room, in whose congenial atmosphere most of this book was written; also, for use of the library's vast and extraordinary facilities and resources, which were at my disposal. These included the A. G. Spalding Collection of Historical Data connected with Baseball; the Bradshaw Hall Swales Collection on Baseball; the original Scrapbooks and Diaries of Henry Chadwick, A. G. Spalding, and Harry Wright; the centuries-old collection of rare manuscripts, newspapers, periodicals, and books; the general and comprehensive reference resources for research; and the generous cooperation and assistance provided by many individuals of the library staff.

I wish also to express particular thanks to my dear wife Isabella, just for "being there" through the years.

Irving A. Leitner

Library of Congress Cataloging in Publication Data

Leitner, Irving A.
　　Baseball: diamond in the rough.

　　1. Baseball—History. I. Title.
GV863.A1L4　　　　796.357'09　　　　70-141561
ISBN 0-200-71792-8

Published on the same day in Canada by Longman Canada Limited.

NEW YORK
Abelard-Schuman
Limited
257 Park Avenue So.

LONDON
Abelard-Schuman
Limited
158 Buckingham Palace Road
SW1W9TR

an Intext *publisher*

Printed in the United States of America

CONTENTS

INTRODUCTION

The year man first set foot on the moon, 1969, was also remarkable in many respects for the American national pastime. It was the year professional baseball celebrated its one hundredth anniversary. It was the year the New York Mets, the most derided team in recent memory, won both the National League pennant and the World Series championship. And it was the year that more than 27 million fans (representing an increase of more than 4 million over the previous year) paid millions upon millions of dollars in admission fees simply to watch a handful of teams compete with one another in the National and American Leagues alone.

In the spring of 1970, the minimum salary for professional big-league players was raised from $10,000 a season to $12,000 ($13,500 by 1972), while the maximum appeared to be nowhere in sight. Salaries of $100,000 and above for star players no longer were considered excessive. St. Louis Cardinal pitcher Bob Gibson, for example, two-time winner of the coveted Cy Young Award, signed his 1971 contract with the Cardinals for $150,000, making him one of the highest paid baseball players in history. And Baltimore slugger Frank Robinson, when asked in 1968 what his demands would be if he were lucky enough to repeat his shining performance of 1966, was reported to have declared, "I wouldn't be ashamed to ask for $200,000. The owners may have ceilings on salaries, but they don't have ceilings on their own salaries or the club profits. If I earn it on the field, I expect to get it." While baseball's beloved Joe DiMaggio, going a step farther, reportedly said that if he were playing today, he not only would ask for $200,000 a year, but he would also get it.

But this phenomenal situation did not always exist in American baseball. There was once an age of innocence, a time of friendly games on open meadows in which spectators lounged and freely watched the teams on the field. There was a time when payments to players or admission fees to ballparks were unknown. And then there were times of change and controversy and scandal.

There was a time in 1879, for instance, when a commentator in a Milwaukee newspaper wrote: "Base ball, it will be remembered by old settlers is a game played by eighteen persons wearing shirts and drawers. They scatter around the field and try to catch a cannon-ball covered with rawhide. The game is to get people to pay two shillings to come inside the fence."

And again, in 1881, when an editorial in *The New York Times* declared: "Our experience with the national game of base-ball has been sufficiently thorough to convince us that it was in the beginning a sport unworthy of men, and that it is now, in its fully developed state, unworthy of gentlemen."

As for player salaries, in 1889, the great slugging first baseman of the Boston Nationals, "Big Dan" Brouthers, received the then impressive sum of $4,700 for the season; Brouthers' teammate, colorful Mike "King" Kelly, received $4,000; and James "Pud" Galvin, the star pitcher of Pittsburgh, $3,000.

And even in this century, in 1911, when the fabulous speedball pitcher Walter Johnson was publicly arguing his case for a salary increase from the Washington club, things were not much better. Johnson said:

> I think that I am worth $7,500 a season to any baseball club . . . I am not making any complaint. This is simply the direct application of the great intelligent American business principle of dog eat dog, the employer trying to get labor for as little as he can, the baseball player trying to get as much as he can for his labor . . . They agree to disagree. Then the employer tries to starve out the laborer, and the laborer tries to ruin the employer's business. They quarrel over a bone and rend each other like coyotes. And we are free-born Americans, with a constitution and public schools. Our business philosophy is that of the wolf pack.

Obviously, the salaries of star professional players have skyrocketed since the times of "King" Kelly and Walter Johnson. Obviously, too, baseball was *not* in its "fully developed state" in 1881, as *The New York Times* then affirmed. Indeed, the condition of the diamond in those early years was highly undeveloped, and it was only through a continuous process of refinement that the national pastime was brought to its present state of affluence.

Interestingly, the growth of professional baseball was spurred by a factor that could only have been dreamed about during the last century, one that had nothing whatever to do with star players, great teams, or even good sportsmanship. That factor was the development of artificial illumination.

O. P. CAYLOR
Nineteenth century sports writer
Speculated in 1893 about the intriguing possibilities of night baseball.

Back in 1893, O. P. Caylor, a sports journalist, toyed with the idea as follows:

> Should the time ever come when by some system of illumination baseball could be played as well at night as in the daytime the possibilities of the game's earnings could hardly be estimated . . . But the chances are that the time will never come when baseball at night will be possible . . . However, it is a subject which will be worth consideration. If any one ever does discover a system of out-of-door lighting sufficiently good for baseball playing in the open air at night he would at once take rank with the millionaires of the land.

How truly prophetic Caylor was can be judged by the fact that not only has night baseball come to pass but also that today major-league games are played more often after dark than in the daytime. For example, during the 1966 season, a total of 1,620 games were played in the National and American Leagues; of these, 861 were night games, while only 759 were day games.

And in 1971, baseball history was made when the fourth game of the World Series took place under the lights. This was the first time in the 68 years of the annual competition that a World Series game was played at night. More than 51,000 spectators—the largest baseball attendance in Pittsburgh annals—watched the home team defeat the Baltimore Orioles by a score of 4 to 3.

Later, the National Broadcasting Company, which had televised the contest, reported that about 63 million individual viewers had watched the game on an estimated 21 million sets. This, according to NBC, was the largest TV audience ever to have watched a sporting event during prime-time evening hours.

But the innovations and drama of baseball are not yet ended. The story of the diamond is a continuing one that flows out of a turbulent and colorful past and that points to an exciting and more brilliant future. This book, it is hoped, will help in some small way to illuminate that heritage of the past which has made the American national pastime the pulsating and dynamic sport that it is.

BASE-BALL SONG

Air: "The Old Oaken Bucket"

How dear to the heart is the green-covered ball-field,
    Where good rival captains their men rightly place,
The pitcher, the catcher, the right field and left field,
    The good men, the true men, who guard well each base!
The short-stop so lively, the centre field handy,
    The ball, and the striker who aims to send high!
But dearer than all to the hearts of good fielders,
    Is the leathern-clad base-ball we catch on the fly—
The jolly old base-ball, the well-covered base-ball,
    The leathern-clad base-ball we catch on the fly.

—Entered in Henry Chadwick's diary,
June 26, 1874.

ONE

◆

RELIGIOUS RITES
AND
PRIMITIVE GAMES

"I asked Khalîl one day to write out for me a list of all the games the boys play in Abeih, and he brought me a list of twenty-eight different ones, and said there were many more." So wrote the American missionary, the Reverend Henry Harris Jessup, reminiscing during the last century about the many years he had spent among the Arabs in Syria before and after the American Civil War.

I. The first is called Khatim or the Ring. A boy puts a ring on the back of his hand, tosses it and catches it on the back of his fingers. If it falls on the middle finger, he shakes it to the forefinger, and then he is Sultan, and appoints a Vizier, whom he commands to beat the other boys. Then the boys all sing:

> *Ding, dong, turn the wheel,*
> *Wind the purple thread:*
> *Spin the white and spin the red,*
> *Wind it on the reel:*
> *Silk and linen as well as you can,*
> *Weave a robe for the Great Sultan.*

II. Killeh. Like the game of shooting marbles.
III. Owal Howa. The same as leap frog . . .
IX. Tabeh. Base ball and drop ball.

It is probable that most Americans will readily accept without question the statement that Arab children over one hundred years ago played games in which they pretended to be sultans and viziers. The idea somehow falls comfortably within the framework of many of our preconceived notions and concepts. But the assertion that Arab boys in a far-off land played Tabeh, or "base ball," during the time that the very first American amateur baseball clubs were being formed may come as a distinct surprise, if not shock. For, historically, baseball has been and is regarded by most of the world as *the* American national pastime.

Indeed, it is believed by many that the game was invented by the American Abner Doubleday, in 1839, and was first played on American soil at Cooperstown, New York.

Nothing could be farther from the truth!

Scholars in recent years have unearthed evidence and advanced theories that seem to indicate, if not prove, that baseball had its origins in other more primitive games played long before 1839 and may even have had its roots as far back as in the days of the secret and mysterious religious fertility rites of ancient Egypt.

Robert W. Henderson, for example, librarian of the Racquet and Tennis Club of New York, and for many years chief of the Main Reading Room of the New York Public Library, Fifth Avenue and Forty-second Street, has presented both convincing arguments and documentary evidence that cast serious doubt on the authenticity of the Doubleday legend. Henderson also has suggested that many different types of ball games, played by various peoples of different lands, have their roots in primitive religious rites of one sort or another.

This theory is supported by a *Memoir* (Number 19) concerning the Shrine of Hathor at the Temple of Deir el Bahari, built about 3,500 years ago. The *Memoir*, written by H. Edouard Naville for the Egypt Exploration Fund, was published in London in 1901.

Naville writes:

I believe the Shrine of Hathor to have been originally a cave where, according to tradition, the queen was suckled by the goddess, and where, at the end of her life, she "joined" her divine nurse. This is why, according to Egyptian ideas, she places her own emblems with those of the goddess, thus deifying herself and claiming the same worship.

Describing the eastern wall of the ante room, Naville informs us:

> Here we have a rare representation, a symbolical ceremony the sense of which is not easy to understand. It is a game of ball. Thothmes III., Menkheperkara, holds a stick of wavy form, which from other texts we know to be made of olive wood, and strikes with it balls, the substance of which we do not know. The ceremony is called: "to strike the ball to (in honour of) Hathor the protectress of Thebes" . . . it is said that the king strikes a ball in honour of his mother. It seems from the text which accompanies the cermony at Dendereh, that the throwing of balls was a kind of emblem of victory, "the enemies are struck before them." There must have been several of them, since we see that the prophets hand them to Thothmes III., or perhaps make the catches.

It is known from inscriptions on the walls of other ancient tombs that games of ball in Egypt, notwithstanding their religious significance, were also played for sport. Depictions of Egyptian women tossing and catching balls have been found. Quantities of wooden "cats," used in the ancient game of "tip-cat," have also been discovered, dating back almost five thousand years.

Joseph Strutt, a British scholar who lived in the latter half of the eighteenth and early part of the nineteenth centuries, described one of the various ways that tip-cat was played by the people of England. He said:

> The method is to make four, six, or eight holes in the ground in a circular direction, and as nearly as possible at equal distances from each other, and at every hole is placed a player with his bludgeon: one of the opposite party who stand in field, tosses the cat to the batsman who is nearest him, and every time the cat is struck the players are obliged to change their situations, and run once from one hole to another in succession; if the cat be driven to any great distance they continue to run in the same order, and claim a score towards their game every time they quit one hole and run to another; but if the cat be stopped by their opponents and thrown across between any two of the holes before the player who has quitted one of them can reach the other, he is out.

Of course the game described is not baseball, nor even one o' cat or two o' cat. However, it requires little imagination to recognize that a certain kinship exists between games in which a bat is used, a tossed object is struck, and players run from base to base or hole to hole.

In fact, it has been suggested that the familiar game one o' cat, sometimes called "one ol' cat" or "one old cat," originally was known as "one *hole* cat." Such a designation would be in perfect harmony with Strutt's description of tip-cat, in which "every time the cat is struck" players "quit one hole and run to another."

The relationship between baseball and one o' cat, two o' cat, etc., is freely admitted. By extension, therefore, it is not inappropriate to include tip-cat within the structural framework of baseball's evolutionary development.

Henderson has asserted in his book *Ball, Bat and Bishop,* and elsewhere, that ball games, connected with certain ancient religious rites of Egypt, somehow found their way into Europe around the ninth and tenth centuries A.D. Subsequently, the Church adopted aspects of the pagan rites and fitted them to Christian religious ceremonies in which a ball was passed about during the course of services, especially around Easter time.

Ball games of various sorts also came to be played in the spring, during the season of nature's rebirth; this paralleled, in time, the celebration by Christians of the Resurrection, which conceivably may be interpreted as a form of spiritual rebirth.

In France, the games of *la soule* and *jeu de paume* achieved wide popularity. These were played, respectively, with bats, feet and ball, and bare palm and ball.

In England, the games of foot-ball, fives, and stool-ball (also known as "tuts") developed.

In both countries, moreover, many of the games were played within the confines of churchyards or in their immediate vicinity.

In fact, so closely were ball games connected with religious influences that clergymen were often seen during the Easter holidays participating in contests with their parishioners.

In an *Admonition to Parliament*, published in 1572, concerning the manner in which ministers conduct church services, Thomas Cartwright wrote the following: "He (the minister) posteth it over as fast as he can galloppe; for, eyther he hath two places to serve; or else there are some games to be playde in the afternoon . . . and, if no place else can be gotten, this interlude must be playde in the church."

In the year 1598, John Stow, a citizen of London, translated from the Latin into English an account of the *Sports and Pastimes of Old Time Used in this City,* written by Fitzstephen in the thirteenth century:

Every year . . . at Shrove Tuesday . . . the schoolboys do bring cocks of the game to their master, and all the forenoon they delight themselves in cock-fighting: after dinner, all the youths go into the fields to play at the ball.

The scholars of every school have their ball, or baton, in their hands; the ancient and wealthy men of the city come forth on horseback to see the sport of the young men, and to take part of the pleasure in beholding their agility.

And some three hundred years after Stow, in 1895, the Reverend Elias Owen shed additional light on conditions as they once had existed in the principality of Wales in Great Britain:

The sports and pastimes of the people in former days took place in churchyards, and when by various means they ceased to be carried on there they ceased altogether. Recreation grounds have not to this day been provided for the people in country places . . . But it is not so long ago that they congregated in the churchyard to test their strength and agility with friendly opponents.

These contests usually took place on the north side of the churchyard, and very often the church wall on that side had no opening, which was very convenient for ball playing, for windows interfered with the free play of the ball, and even when church restorations took place, and the dead wall gave place to windows, shutters were set up, which were closed whilst the game was going on.

In the course of his discussion, the Reverend Owen also illuminated an old and little known Welsh custom that today may surprise and perhaps chagrin some conservative, temperance-minded people while delighting other more indulgent individuals. Indeed, during certain periods in the course of baseball's development, the Welsh practice would have been roundly condemned:

Games—even Sunday games—in churchyards, often created thirst, but as in many cases there was a public-house with a door opening into the churchyard, there was no difficulty in procuring a supply of beer for the players. Indeed, in old churches there usually was a small recess in the church wall large enough to contain a quart jug, which was always kept replenished with the publican's good home brewed ale. This hole was called in Welsh the *Twll chwart*, or the Quart-hole.

Curiously, an American newspaper report of July 1882, from the Harrisburg *Patriot*, although not concerned with ancient Welsh churchyard games, nevertheless bore a distinct spiritual kinship to them. The dispatch read as follows:

A novel game of base ball was played at Conshohocken by rival clubs of Connaughtown. A keg of beer was placed on third base, and a rule prescribed that no player could have a drink until he reached that station. The effect was singular. Every player reached the third base, and so frequently that two kegs were emptied before the game was half over.

TWO

FROM

STOOL-BALL

TO

BASEBALL

The precise origins of the modern game of baseball are heavily shrouded by the almost impenetrable veils of the past. Consequently, any attempt to pinpoint specifically the exact moment of transition between one ancient game and another and to say that this is where or how baseball began is at best a tricky and controversial business.

Nevertheless, certain conclusions may be reached by carefully weighing and examining the information that is available, the historical facts that are indisputable, and the logical probabilities of occurrence.

Adopting this avenue of approach, it may be stated that one of the logical probabilities is the likelihood that the direct and immediate ancestor of baseball is the English children's game of rounders.

Rounders, of all the known variations of bat-and-ball games, bears the closest resemblance to the early game of baseball. In fact, the so-called "Massachusetts Game" or "New England Game of Base Ball," as it was later called, was nothing more than the English game of rounders under a different name.

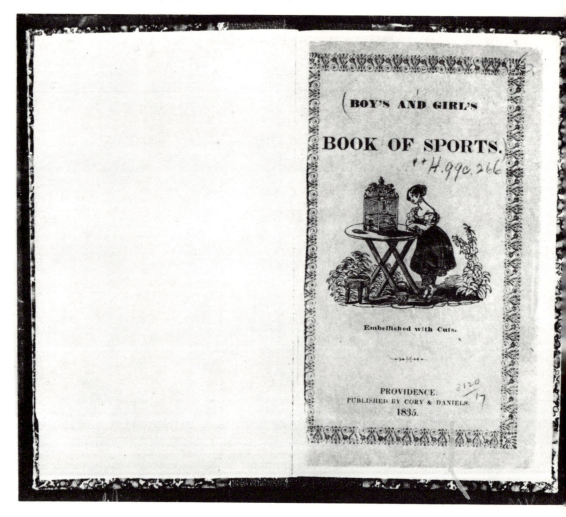

Indeed, the first description of "Base, or Goal Ball," known to have been printed in this country (in Boston, 1834) was simply an almost word-for-word copy of the rules for rounders, which appeared five years earlier in a compact little volume entitled *The Boy's Own Book,* otherwise described as "A Popular Encyclopedia of the Sports and Pastimes of Youth, —a companion for all holydays," compiled by William Clarke and published in London by Vizetelly, Branston & Co.

the wall, but fails to hit it, and the other player catches it before it twice touches the ground, the first boy loses his innings and the other takes his place—and thus the game goes on.

Base, or Goal Ball.—In Base, the players divide themselves into two equal parties, and chance decides which shall have first innings. Four stones or stakes are placed from twelve to twenty yards asunder, as, *a,* c b, c, d, in the margin; another is put B D at e. One of the party, who is out, E places himself at c. He tosses the a ball gently toward *a,* in front of whom one of the *in-party* places himself, who strikes the ball, if possible, with his bat. If he miss three times, or if the ball, when struck, be caught by any of the players of the opposite side, who are scattered about the field, he is out, and another takes his place. If none of these accidents take place, on striking the ball he drops the bat, and runs toward *b,* or, if he can, to *c, d,* or even to *a,* again. If, however, the boy who stands at *c,* or any of the out-players who may happen to have the ball, strike him with it in his progress from *a* to *b, b* to *c, c* to *d,* or *d* to *a,* he is out. Supposing he can only get to *b,* one of his partners takes the bat, and strikes at the ball in turn. If the first player can only get to *c,* or *d,* the second runs to *b,* only, or *c,* as the case may be, and a third

player begins; as they get home, that is, to *a,* they play at the ball by turns, until they all get out. Then, of course, the out-players take their places.

Nine Holes.—Near a wall where the ground is level, dig nine, or a less number of holes, according to the number of players, large enough for a ball to be rolled in without difficulty. Number them, and let each player be allotted a number, by chance, or choice as it may be agreed. A line is drawn about five yards from the holes, at which one of the players places himself, and rolls the ball into one of the holes. The player to whom the hole, into which the ball is rolled, belongs, picks it up as quickly as he can, and endeavors to hit one of the others with it. The latter all run off as soon as they perceive that the ball is not in their holes. If the thrower miss his aim, he loses a point, and it is his turn to roll. If, however, he hit another, he loses nothing; but the party hit becomes the loser, and it is his turn to roll.

TOPS.

Humming Tops, of various sizes, may be bought at the toy-shops. Very little art is necessary to use them. After the string is wound about the upright piece, one end of it is taken in one hand, and the handle of the fork-piece in the other; the string is then to be pulled off with force, and the top is set up.

1835 description of *Base, or Goal Ball.*

Robin Carver was the author of the American book, *The Book of Sports,* which contained the pirated playing rules for rounders, rechristened by him, "Base, or Goal Ball."

Robert W. Henderson was the first to point out the remarkable identity between the descriptions of the two differently named games in the two different volumes.

In addition, Henderson also called attention to the fact that Carver's description was distinguished by the addition of a clever line drawing the caption of which read, "Playing Ball." The drawing showed a group of boys at play on Boston Common, which setting was selected, no doubt, to lend an American character to the game.

Pages from a work published by Samuel Wood & Sons, 1820.

The revelation that the same game was known by a different name in a different geographical location, however, is not a surprising discovery in itself. Even in the description of rounders contained in *The Boy's Own Book*, Clarke states, "In the metropolis, (London), boys play a game very similar to it, called Feeder."

And for that matter, the primitive game of baseball, or variations of

CHILDREN'S AMUSEMENTS. 9

PLAYING ball is much practised by school boys, and is an excellent exercise to unbend the mind, and restore to the body that elasticity and spring which the close application to sedentary employment in their studies within doors, has a tendency to clog, dull or blunt. But when practised as is the common method, with a club or bat great care is necessary, as some times sad accidents have happened, by its slipping from the hand, or hitting some of their fellows. We would therefore, recommend. Fives as a safer play, in which the club is not used and which is equally good for exercise. The writer of this, beside other sad hurts which he has been witness of in the use of clubs, knew a youth who had his skull broke badly with one, and it nearly cost him his life.

it, had been known by sundry other names as well, including the following: town-ball, base-ball, poisoned ball, barn-ball, house-ball, round ball, Boston ball, etc.

Moreover, the discovery that Carver simply copied Clarke's description of rounders is not as astonishing as it may seem. The practice by one writer or book publisher of pirating the literary works of another writer or publisher was quite common at the time.

Indeed, *The Boy's Own Book*—the very work from which Robin Carver copied the description of rounders—contains descriptions of other games that William Clarke copied practically word for word from Joseph Strutt's work of almost a generation before—*The Sports and Pastimes of the People of England.*

Some of Clarke's "borrowings" that fall into this category include descriptions of the games of tip-cat; goff, or bandy-ball; stool-ball; northern-spell; etc.

Also, it would be interesting to ascertain, if possible, whether Clarke's description of rounders was actually original with him, or whether that, too, was "borrowed" from some other unknown author's work.

The matter, therefore, boils down to this: The real importance of Henderson's discovery regarding Carver and Clarke lies mainly in the fact that it provided the first detailed documentary evidence in the English language of a transitional link between baseball and a previously known, similarly played, bat-and-ball game—rounders.

Even so, the possibility should not be lost sight of that similar or identical phenomena may arise independently of one another at the same or different times in various parts of the world. A case in point exists in connection with the very game of rounders, from which baseball appears to have been immediately derived.

In the year 1900, the *Memoirs* of the American Museum of Natural History were published concerning the Jesup North Pacific Expedition of 1897. One of the *Memoirs*, written by James Teit, described the customs and habits of the Thompson Indians of British Columbia, who had up to that time very little contact with white men and whose population then numbered about seven hundred individuals.

Regarding the tribe's recreations, this is what Teit wrote:

Formerly* a favorite pastime was playing ball. The ball used was a kind of knot found on fir-trees. This knot was nicely rounded off, and sometimes covered with buckskin. Other balls were of stone, or of deerskin stuffed with vegetable material . . . The bat used in this game was a short straight stick about four inches wide at one end. Each side took turns in batting. Four stones were placed about twenty yards apart, in the form of a square. These were called "houses." The man who held the bat was bowled to by a man of the opposite party. If he struck the ball with his bat, he immediately dropped the latter, and ran to the first house, or the second if he could manage it. The object of the opposite party was to catch the ball as quickly as

* This could mean as early as 1858, when the first white men arrived in the area.

possible, and strike the man with it while he was running from one house to the other, thereby knocking him out of the game. If the man managed to get back to his starting-point, he was allowed another chance to bat. This game is still frequently played by the young men.

To all intents and purposes, judging from Teit's description, it may be said that the Thompson Indians of British Columbia played a game in the nineteenth century remarkably like the English game of rounders, from which the American game of baseball appears to have been derived.

Taking the probabilities of occurrence into consideration, however, it hardly seems likely that the American game stems from a primitive ball game played by a small Canadian tribe of Indians. Yet, oddly enough, a clipping from the year 1887, pasted in the scrapbook of Henry Chadwick, known as the "Father of Baseball," lends support to the claim for a Canadian origin of the game. The clipping reads as follows:

> In a lengthy letter to the Sporting Life, of Philadelphia, Dr. Ford, of Denver, Colorado, shows that the game of baseball—usually called the national game of the United States—really originated in Canada. He cites an instance of his witnessing a game on the 4th of June, 1838, at Beachville, Ontario, between the local club and the Zorras, from Zorra and North Oxford. Among those who took part in the game were: Geo. Burdick, Reuben Martin, Adam Karn, Wm. Autchinson, I. Van Alstine, Peter Karn, "Old Ned" Dolson, Nathaniel McNames, Abel and John Williams, Harry and Daniel Karn, Wm. Ford and Wm. Dodge. Dr. Ford also mentions in connection with the game at that time the names of Neil McTaggart, Henry Crittenden, Gordon Cook, Henry Taylor, James Piper, Almon Burtch and Wm. Harrington. He closes his communication with the statement that he has played from that day to this, and does not intend to quit as long as there is another boy on the ground.

Despite the existence of these two unconnected, yet geographically related pieces of evidence, the weight of probability is against the conclusion that baseball, as we know it, had its origins north of the American border.

Other and prior evidence exists—as Henderson has pointed out—that a bat-and-ball game called Base-Ball was known in England at least as early as 1744, in which year a book containing a rhyme about such a game was published in that country by the renowned British publisher of books for children, John Newberry. The work, *A Little Pretty Pocket-Book,* contained a small illustration of children playing the game.

Newberry's book apparently achieved wide popularity, for over the years many editions were printed in Great Britain; by 1787 at least three editions had been pirated by American publishers.

Other known references to baseball, by that specific name, exist in the writings of British subjects of the eighteenth century. It is more than likely that additional references that are unknown also exist; and it is probable that those will be revealed in the course of time.

The linkage between American baseball and English rounders, however, appears to be well established. By examining earlier English ball games, it is possible to support still further the theory of baseball's British-American evolutionary development.

In particular, the medieval game of stool-ball (previously mentioned in connection with early English churchyard games) appears to be the direct forerunner of the game of rounders. A brief description will make the relationship apparent.

In 1801, Joseph Strutt provided us with the following:

> I have been informed, that a pastime called stool-ball, is practised to this day in the northern parts of England, which consists in simply setting a stool upon the ground, and one of the players takes his place before it, while his antagonist, standing at a distance, tosses a ball with the intention of striking the stool; and this it is the business of the former to prevent by beating it away with the hand, reckoning one to the game for every stroke of the ball; if, on the contrary, it should be missed by the hand and touch the stool, the players change places;

At this point, Strutt inserted the following footnote: "I believe the same also happens if the person who threw the ball can catch and retain it when driven back, before it reaches the ground."

Then, continuing:

> The conqueror at this game is he who strikes the ball most times before it touches the stool. Again, in other parts of the country a certain number of stools are set up in a circular form, and at a distance from each other, and every one of them is occupied by a single player; when the ball is struck, which is done as before with the hand, they are every one of them obliged to alter his situation, running in succession from stool to stool, and if he who threw the ball can regain it in time to strike any one of the players, before he reaches the stool to which he is running, he takes his place, and the person touched must throw the ball, until he can in like manner return to the circle.

THE ANCIENT NATIONAL GAME OF STOOLBALL—A MATCH AT HORSHAM PARK.
From *The Graphic*, October 12th, 1878.

It is obvious in the description above that by substituting a bat for the hand, and stones, posts or bases for the stools, the game described very easily could be mistaken for a form of rounders.

It is also of further interest to note that Strutt maintains that stool-ball seems to have been played mostly by women rather than by men, although, occasionally, he says the game was played by the youth of both sexes. That this latter contention was indeed so is borne out by a four-line verse that appeared among the observations for the month of April in Poor Robin's *Almanack* for 1677, a century and a quarter before Strutt:

> *Young men and maids,*
> *Now very brisk*
> *At barley-break and*
> *Stool ball frisk.*

In any event, with the establishment of the British colonies in the New World and the arrival at these shores of multitudes of British settlers, many English sports and pastimes found their way to American soil, including the base-running, bat-and-ball games of stool-ball, cricket, and rounders—whence came the modern game of baseball.

Stool-ball, in fact, bears the added distinction of having been the first known sport of its kind to have been played here by white men—the game having been played, early in the seventeenth century, by the Pilgrims in Plymouth.

However, from stool-ball to baseball as we know it, there lay a trying and difficult period of aging, growth, and development. But grow and develop it did—so much so, that today it can be meaningfully said that baseball is the American national pastime.

THREE

THE FIRST
BASEBALL CLUBS

The honors for having been the first regularly organized club to play baseball usually are bestowed on the Knickerbocker Base Ball Club of New York, which officially came into existence on September 23, 1845.

However, other clubs are known to have existed before that date, whose members also played the game, or variations of it, yet never really organized themselves into formal clubs.

One such outfit, for example, was composed of a group of town ball enthusiasts who played during the seasons of 1831 and 1832 on the grounds at Market Street, Philadelphia. Another such group played the game at about the same time just across the Delaware River in Camden, New Jersey.

A nineteenth-century account reads:

The first day that the Philadelphia men took the field . . . only four men were found to play, so they started in by playing a game called cat ball. All the players were over 25 years of age, and to see them playing a game like this caused much merriment among the friends of the players. It required "sand" in those days to go out on the field and play, as the prejudice against the game was very great. It took nearly a whole season to get men enough together to make a team, owing to the ridicule heaped upon the players for taking part in such childish sports.

The Philadelphia athletes, however, apparently had the necessary "sand," for, despite the public ridicule, they continued to meet and play, although they had no organized club as such, no formal playing rules, and no regular playing field.

Finally, in 1833, the situation changed; for in that year, the players from Camden joined up with the Philadelphia men, and together they formed the Olympic Town Ball Club of Philadelphia.

The Olympics, so far as can be ascertained, were the first known team of its type in the United States, and its members played town ball among themselves for many years after their formation.

Playing equipment presented no problem to the club, financial or otherwise; most players at the time made their own bats and balls, and regular playing uniforms were not used.

The ball usually consisted of an artfully wound sphere of yarn covered with leather that was cut in three segments and sewn together by hand with waxed shoemaker's thread and awl.

The bat used was one of two types, the choice depending on whether the striker (as the batter was called) used two hands or one when striking the ball.

If the striker used two hands, the bat was broad and flat, closely resembling a cricket bat. If he used one hand, the bat was shaped like a miniature baseball bat and was called a "delill."

A good player was able to use either type.

However, when "delilling," the striker, instead of swinging at the ball, would simply allow the ball to be deflected off his bat, directing it to whatever area of the playing field he chose by holding the delill at a given angle.

The Olympic playing field itself was actually an open space in which a square had been marked off with corners or "bases" placed about sixty feet apart. The batter stood midway between the first and fourth corners, and the catcher was positioned behind the batter, beyond the demarcation line of the square. No set number of men made up a team.

Besides the Olympics, various other town ball teams played sporadically in the Philadelphia area, but these either quickly disbanded or their players were absorbed into the original Olympic Club. The public prejudice that had prevailed from the start against grown men playing what was regarded as a young boys' game continued for a number of years; and this, in large measure, prevented the formation and survival of other formally organized town ball clubs.

But if town ball for adult players was meeting with public disfavor in the Quaker City in the 1830s, by the following decade, its closely related pastime, baseball, was encountering fashionable acceptance in New York.

Charles A. Peverelly, the noted "Out-Door Sports" journalist of the period, recorded it in 1866 as follows:

> During the years of 1842 and '43, a number of gentlemen, fond of the game, casually assembled on a plot of ground in Twenty-seventh street . . . bringing with them their bats, balls, etc. It was customary for two or three players, occasionally during the season, to go around in the forenoon of a pleasant day and muster up players enough to make a match . . . Among the prominent players were Col. James Lee, Dr. Ransom, Abraham Tucker, James Fisher, W. Vail . . . In the spring of 1845 Mr. Alex. J. Cartwright . . . one day upon the field proposed a regular organization . . . His proposal was acceded to, and Messrs. W. R. Wheaton, Cartwright, D. F. Curry, E. R. Dupignac, Jr., and W. H. Tucker, formed themselves into a board of recruiting officers, and soon obtained names enough to make a respectable show . . . Thus it occurred that a party of gentlemen formed an organization, combining together health, recreation, and social enjoyment, which was the nucleus of the now great American game of Base Ball, so popular in all parts of the United States, than which there is none more manly or more health-giving.

The "organization" formed by that "party of gentlemen" was none other than the pioneer Knickerbocker Base Ball Club of New York. Shortly afterward, the Knickerbockers went "prospecting" for a regular playing area, and this led them across the Hudson River to the Elysian Fields, a large grassy meadow in Hoboken, New Jersey, where they "settled."

Commenting on the Knickerbocker membership, Peverelly wrote: "Its members have from its inception been composed mostly of those whose sedentary habits required recreation, and its respectability has ever been undoubted . . . no person can obtain admission in the club merely for his capacity as a player; he must also have the reputation of a gentleman."

Clearly, Peverelly's repetitive use of such words and phrases as "gentlemen," "prominent players," "sedentary habits," and "respectability" all indicate that the Knickerbocker Club actually was an exclusive, upper-leisure-class affair, whose members constituted a sort of exercise-seeking social aristocracy.

The words of King James I of Great Britain, addressed around the turn of the sixteenth century to his eldest son Henry, the Prince of Wales, as well as to his court in general, are brought to mind:

Certainly, bodily exercises and games are very commendable, as well
for banishing of Idleness, the mother of all vice; as for making the body
able and durable for travell, which is very necessarie for a king. But
from this court I debarre all rough and violent exercises; as the
foote-ball, meeter for lameing, than making able, the users thereof; as
likewise such tumbling trickes as only serve for comoedians and
balladines to win their bread with: but the exercises that I would
have you to use, although but moderately, not making a craft of them,
are, running, leaping, wrestling, fencing, dancing, and playing at
the caitch . . .

Original Rules of the Knickerbocker Base Ball Club
Adopted September 23, 1845

1st.—Members must strictly observe the time agreed upon for exercise,
and be punctual in their attendance.

2d.—When assembled for exercise, the President, or in his absence
the Vice-President, shall appoint an Umpire, who shall keep the game
in a book provided for that purpose, and note all violations of the
By-Laws and Rules during the time of exercise.

3d.—The presiding officer shall designate two members as Captains,
who shall retire and make the match to be played, observing at the
same time that the players put opposite to each other should be as
nearly equal as possible; the choice of sides to be then tossed for,
and the *first in hand* to be decided in like manner.

4th.—The bases shall be from "home" to second base, forty-two paces;
from first to third base, forty-two paces, equidistant.

5th.—No stump match shall be played on a regular day of exercise.

6th.—If there should not be a sufficient number of members of the
Club present at the time agreed upon to commence exercise, gentlemen
not members may be chosen in to make up the match, which *shall
not be broken up* to take in members that may afterwards appear; but,
in all cases, members shall have the preference, when present, at
the making of a match.

7th.—If members appear after the game is commenced they may be
chosen in if mutually agreed upon.

8th.—The game to consist of twenty-one counts, or aces; but at the
the conclusion an equal number of hands must be played.

Of course, the members of the Knickerbocker Club were not members of the court of King James I, but in their own "aristocratic" way, "not making a craft" of baseball, they recognized the value of "bodily exercises" and "playing at the caitch."

Indeed, judging from the manner in which the game was referred to in the official rules of the club, the conclusion may be clearly drawn that baseball was regarded by the members not really as a sport, rather as a form of exercise. Note, in particular, Rules 1, 2, 5, and 6.

9th.—The ball must be pitched, and not thrown, for the bat.

10th.—A ball knocked out the field, or outside the range of the first or third base, is foul.

11th.—Three balls being struck at and missed and the last one caught, is a hand out; if not caught is considered fair, and the striker bound to run.

12th.—If a ball be struck, or tipped, and caught, either flying or on the first bound, it is a hand out.

13th.—A player running the bases shall be out, if the ball is in the hands of an adversary on the base, or the runner is touched with it before he makes his base; it being understood, however, that in no instance is a ball to be thrown at him.

14th.—A player running who shall prevent an adversary from catching or getting the ball before making his base, is a hand out.

15th.—Three hands out, all out.

16th.—Players must take their strike in regular turn.

17th.—All disputes and differences relative to the game, to be decided by the Umpire, from which there is no appeal.

18th.—No ace or base can be made on a foul strike.

19th.—A runner cannot be put out in making one base, when a balk is made by the pitcher.

20th.—But one base allowed when a ball bounds out of the field when struck.

William R. Wheaton,
William H. Tucker,
Committee on By-Laws.

Further indication that the game was regarded essentially as an exercise rather than a sport is provided by two sections of Article VII of the By-Laws, concerned with fines and penalties. The sections read as follows:

> SECTION 7.—Any member disputing the decision of an umpire during the time of *exercise*, shall be fined twenty-five cents for each offence.

> SECTION 10.—All fines incurred by violation of any of the four preceding sections must be paid to the Captains immediately after play, and any member refusing to pay such fines shall be suspended from field *exercise*, till such fines are paid.*

It may further be observed that if Section 10 is to be taken at its face value, it would seem that the Knickerbocker Base Ball Club was not overly inclined to extend financial credit to its members, even to the extent of a dime, which was the penalty levied under Section 6: "Members using profane or improper language on the field, shall be fined ten cents for each offence."

This was hardly the way to treat gentlemen, or for that matter, considering the offense, for gentlemen to behave. But, apparently, these particular sections of the By-Laws simply recognized that all men, even gentlemen, are subject to human frailties.

Indeed, the Excelsior Base Ball Club of Brooklyn, a later organization, went even further than the Knickerbockers. One of the Excelsior By-Laws required a member to have "*written* permission" before "wearing or using the apparel of a fellow-member." The penalty for infraction of this rule was a fine of one dollar.

The first recorded match of the Knickerbocker Base Ball Club was a brief four-inning contest, played at the Elysian Fields, Hoboken, on June 19, 1846. The opposing team was composed of selected members of the New York Base Ball Club, an outfit said to have been in existence before the Knickerbockers, but on an unorganized basis.

The contest was a most embarrassing affair for the Knickerbockers, for they lost the match by the score of 23 to 1. Had the New York team scored their 23 runs in less than four innings, the match would have been an even briefer event than it was, since according to Rule 8, under which the match was played, the first team to score "twenty-one counts, or aces," playing "an equal number of hands," won the game.

The box score of that historic match read as follows:

* Italics are the author's.

KNICKERBOCKER CLUB		NEW YORK CLUB	
Turney	1 out, 0 runs.	Davis	1 out, 3 runs.
Adams	1 out, 0 runs.	Winslow	2 outs, 2 runs.
Tucker	2 outs, 0 runs.	Ransom	2 outs, 3 runs.
Birney	1 out, 1 run.	Murphy	0 outs, 4 runs.
Avery	0 outs, 0 runs.	Case	0 outs, 4 runs.
H. Anthony	2 outs, 0 runs.	Johnson	1 out, 2 runs.
D. Anthony	2 outs, 0 runs.	Thompson	2 outs, 2 runs.
Tryon	2 outs, 0 runs.	Trenchard	2 outs, 1 run.
Paulding	1 out, 0 runs.	Lalor	2 outs, 2 runs.
Total 12 outs, 1 run.		**Total 12 outs, 23 runs.**	

In 1849, the Knickerbockers adopted an official uniform for the club, which consisted of "blue woollen pantaloons, white flannel shirt," and "chip (straw) hats." Six years later, a broad patent-leather belt was added, while the straw hats gave way to mohair caps. Blue and white, however, continued to be the official colors of the club.

At the start of the second half of the century, a rash of amateur clubs, modeled on the Knickerbockers, suddenly sprang into existence, one after another. Some of these, with the year of their organization, were the following:

Gotham—1850
Empire—1854
Putnam, Baltic, Eckford, Union, Atlantic of Jamaica—1855
Harlem, Enterprise, Atlantic of Brooklyn—1856
Mutual, Oriental, Pastime—1857

The Elysian Fields, Hoboken, was the scene of most matches involving the Knickerbocker, Gotham, and Empire clubs; playing sites of other clubs included the grounds in South Brooklyn; 86th Street and Second Avenue; Greenpoint, Long Island; Woodstock; Jamaica; and 123rd Street and Fifth Avenue.

The first newspaper report of a baseball match known to have been printed in this country appeared in the New York *Mercury* of July 10, 1853. The item was written by William Cauldwell, one of the *Mercury* proprietors; in its entirety, it read as follows: "Baseball.—The Gotham and Knickerbocker clubs played a match game, on the grounds of the latter, at Hoboken, on the 5th inst. The Knickerbockers won. Gotham, 18 outs, 12 runs; Knickerbocker, 18 outs, 21 runs—21 runs constituting a game."

EAGLES AND GOTHAMS AT ELYSIAN FIELDS, HOBOKEN, N.J., SEPTEMBER 1857.
From Porter's *Spirit of the Times.*

With the press finally taking notice, baseball clubs as such received an important form of recognition. However, that games were being played and young men were watching was often the only stimulus needed for the formation of a club. The Excelsiors, for example, were organized shortly after John H. Suydam and several of his friends witnessed a game between the Knickerbockers and the Eagles in the fall of 1854.

"Why don't we 'get up' a club of our own?" they thought—and they did. The young men met for informal practice several days later, calling themselves the "J.Y.B.B.B.C.," which stood for "Jolly Young Bachelors' Base Ball Club."

Committees were then appointed to draw up a constitution and bylaws, and on December 8, 1854, a formal meeting was held at which the "young bachelors" accepted the committee reports and adopted the official name by which they came to be known—the Excelsior Club.

That a game between the Knickerbockers and the Eagles should have inspired the organization of the famous Excelsior Club is an interesting historical sidelight. However, a much more fascinating situation exists with regard to these two clubs, the ramifications of which could conceivably alter the generally accepted conclusion that the Knickerbockers were the first organized amateur baseball club in America.

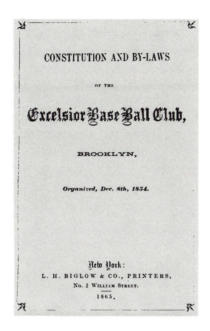

Pages from the By-Laws of the Excelsior Base Ball Club.
Note the use of the term "field exercise" instead of "baseball game."

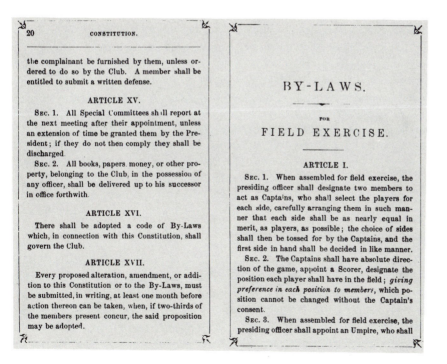

20   CONSTITUTION.

the complainant be furnished by them, unless ordered to do so by the Club. A member shall be entitled to submit a written defense.

ARTICLE XV.

SEC. 1. All Special Committees shall report at the next meeting after their appointment, unless an extension of time be granted them by the President; if they do not then comply they shall be discharged.

SEC. 2. All books, papers, money, or other property, belonging to the Club, in the possession of any officer, shall be delivered up to his successor in office forthwith.

ARTICLE XVI.

There shall be adopted a code of By-Laws which, in connection with this Constitution, shall govern the Club.

ARTICLE XVII.

Every proposed alteration, amendment, or addition to this Constitution or to the By-Laws, must be submitted, in writing, at least one month before action thereon can be taken, when, if two-thirds of the members present concur, the said proposition may be adopted.

BY-LAWS.

FOR

FIELD EXERCISE.

ARTICLE I.

SEC. 1. When assembled for field exercise, the presiding officer shall designate two members to act as Captains, who shall select the players for each side, carefully arranging them in such manner that each side shall be as nearly equal in merit, as players, as possible; the choice of sides shall then be tossed for by the Captains, and the first side in hand shall be decided in like manner.

SEC. 2. The Captains shall have absolute direction of the game, appoint a Scorer, designate the position each player shall have in the field; *giving preference in each position to members*, which position cannot be changed without the Captain's consent.

SEC. 3. When assembled for field exercise, the presiding officer shall appoint an Umpire, who shall

Title page from the By-Laws of the Eagle Base Ball Club.

By-Laws of the Eagle Ball Club.

ARTICLE I.—THE CLUB.

§ 1. THIS Club shall be designated by the name of the "EAGLE BALL CLUB."

§ 2. The Club shall consist of not more than forty members.

§ 3. Honorary members may be elected by an unanimous vote.

ARTICLE II.—MEMBERSHIP.

§ 1. Gentlemen wishing to become members may be proposed at any regular meeting, and at the next regular meeting be balloted for.

§ 2. At a ballot for membership two nays shall exclude the applicant.

§ 3 Gentlemen becoming members must sign the By-Laws of the Club, and furnish the Secretary with their place of residence.

§ 4. Any member wishing to withdraw from the Club, must offer his resignation at a regular meeting ; but no resignation shall be accepted if the member be in arrears.

ARTICLE III.—MEETINGS.

§ 1. The meetings of the Club shall be held quarterly, that is the second Wednesday in February, May, August and November of each year, at 8 o'clock, P. M.

In the 1861 issue of *Beadle's Dime Base-Ball Player* (edited by Henry Chadwick), the following statement appears: "There was a Club called the New York Club, which existed before the Knickerbocker, but we shall not be far wrong if we award to the latter club the honor of being the pioneer of the present game of Base Ball."

Later, in 1866, Charles A. Peverelly, Chadwick's colleague, wrote: "The Eagle Base Ball Club, of New York, was organized in the Spring of 1854 . . . The Eagles rank as the third base ball club of the country in their institution; and it is no eulogy to say of them that, in all the attributes of a solid, respectable, and honorable organization, they are second to none."

Here, then, we have a situation in which the so-called Father of Baseball, Henry Chadwick, gives qualified credit ("we shall not be far wrong") to the Knickerbockers (organized in 1845) for having been the first baseball club of its kind in America, while Charles A. Peverelly, the other distinguished sports journalist of the period, states unequivocally that the Eagle Club "was organized in the Spring of 1854."

Still, among the millions of volumes owned by the New York Public Library, Fifth Avenue and 42nd Street, there exists a tiny volume entitled "By-Laws and Rules of the Eagle Ball Club," published in New York by Douglass & Colt, Printers, in the year 1852, two years before Peverelly claims the club was organized.

And still further, in the center of the title page, under the name of the club, there appears the following: "Organized, 1840." This date, of course, is five years earlier than 1845, the year the Knickerbocker Club, the hitherto regarded "pioneer" baseball club, was organized.

Since myths and legends abound in baseball—as has so often been noted—the significance of all this will not be speculated on in these pages. The facts speak for themselves.

A stinger.
The Knickerbocker rules
made this form of out illegal.

FOUR

◆

THE NEW YORK GAME
vs.
THE MASSACHUSETTS GAME

Come, base ball players all and listen to the song
About our manly Yankee game, and pardon what is wrong;
If the verses do not suit you, I hope the chorus will,
So join with us, one and all, and sing it with a will.

—From the song sung at
the Knickerbocker supper
honoring the Excelsiors, 1858.

As more and more baseball clubs made their appearance in the fifties and more and more contests were played, it soon became apparent that some sort of uniformity of playing rules and regulations was needed both to govern the games themselves and to stabilize relations among the various clubs.

In the New York area, this need was met by the issuance of a call, in 1856, by the officers of the Knickerbocker Club for a convention to be held at which representatives of the clubs could draw up a permanent baseball code to regulate the growing sport.

As a consequence, the first convention of baseball players was convened in New York City in May 1857. Thirty-two delegates attended, representing the following sixteen clubs: Knickerbocker, Gotham, Empire, Eagle, Excelsior, Putnam, Baltic, Atlantic, Eckford, Union, Harlem, Harmony, Bedford, Olympic, Nassau, and Continental.

This first convention was a cordial meeting and set the stage for the second, which was held the following year, on March 10, 1858, also in New York City.

The second convention, attended by delegates from twelve additional clubs, distinguished itself by creating the first baseball association in history—the National Association of Base Ball Players. A regular constitution and a set of bylaws were drawn up; these were adopted by the delegates; and it was decided to make the convention a permanent annual event. One year later, on March 19, 1859, the National Association of Base Ball Players held its first annual meeting at Cooper Institute, New York.

And from all this, the so-called "New York Game" was born, which marked the advent of "modern" baseball.

It might be recalled at this juncture that it was the Knickerbocker Base Ball Club that first adopted—in 1845—a formal code of playing rules. Rule 13 of that original code marked the point of departure from the more primitive game of rounders in which wooden stakes stood for bases and a player was put out by being struck with the ball.

Rule 13 of the Knickerbocker code declared a runner out "if the ball is in the hands of an adversary on the base, or the runner is touched with it before he makes his base;" but the basic and most important new element in the game as played by the Knickerbockers was that "in no instance is a ball to be thrown at" the runner.

Since, as a necessary feature of the game, a player no longer could be deliberately hit with the ball, the danger of thereby wounding him was eliminated. This, in turn, made it possible to use a harder ball than heretofore, which substitution (hard ball for soft ball) changed the nature of the game.

Because a hard ball travels much farther and more swiftly when struck than does a soft ball, it became necessary for the fielders to develop greater skill and more efficient teamwork to put an opposing player out. This had the desirable effect of making the game, at one and the same time, faster, more interesting, and more scientific.

The new playing technique, introduced by the Knickerbockers, became fundamental in the New York Game, for the principle was incorporated in the rules and regulations adopted by the National Association of Base Ball Players, to which most of the clubs in the New York area adhered.

Of course, in addition to this particular feature, the National Association code had much greater scope than the original Knickerbocker rules, for the various other specifications of the game were much more carefully spelled out. And over the years, through sundry changes, improvements, and additions to the basic playing rules and regulations, a governing code was developed that gradually was adopted by baseball clubs throughout the nation.

The innovations wrought by the development of the New York Game, under the guidance of the National Association of Base Ball Players, were briefly summarized in an article copyrighted in 1888 by J. F. Spofford & Co. They read as follows:

> The diamond supplanted the square; canvas bases supplanted stakes; a pitched ball took the place of a thrown ball; nine innings, and not a certain number of runs, constituted a game; three men, and not one man, put the side out; nine players constituted a side; the base runner could not be put out on a thrown ball . . . however, a catch of a fair bound or of a foul bound disposed of the batsman.* Otherwise . . . the base runner could not run three feet out of the line of base; he could not score from third after two men were out if the batter had not reached first base safely; in case of rain, at least five innings constituted a game, and the distances between bases were 45 feet.

In the 1850s, naturally enough, the greatest exponents of the New York Game were the teams playing in the vicinity of New York. Brooklyn, of course, fell within that category. And even as Brooklyn and New York are traditional rivals today, so they were over one hundred years ago, when each community was a separate city.

During that period, when the New York Game was coming into its own, the city of New York boasted at least four prominent baseball clubs— the Knickerbocker, Gotham, Eagle, and Empire.

So, too, did the city of Brooklyn, whose leading clubs were the Excelsior, Atlantic, Putnam, and Eckford.

In 1858, a three-match series was proposed and agreed on to determine the baseball championship of the two cities. The best players were

---

* In 1864, this rule was changed and the "fly catch" out was adopted instead.

selected from among the various teams of each city; two representative teams were formed; and on July 20, 1858, the first contest of a series ever played for a baseball championship took place on the grounds of the Fashion Race Course, located near Jamaica, Long Island. (The competition ultimately became known as the "Fashion Course Contests.")

The first match resulted in a victory for New York, by a four-run margin; the final score was 22 to 18. In the second match, the Brooklyn team evened the series by the score of 29 to 8; but in the final contest, the New Yorkers came back to triumph, 29 to 18, thereby capturing the first baseball championship ever to have been contested.

At about the same time that the New York Game was gaining acceptance all over the nation, in one area, at least—New England—the old style of play was being clung to tenaciously. There, particularly in the state of Massachusetts, the type of baseball most closely akin to town ball and rounders appeared to have its deepest roots. Indeed, the old game even seemed to flourish for a number of years and became known, in contrast to the New York Game, as the Massachusetts Game.

The first baseball club regularly organized in the state of Massachusetts was the Olympic Club of Boston, formed in 1854. During its first year of existence, it was the sole club of its kind. Then, in 1855, the Elm Tree Club was organized, with whose team the Olympics played their first match. However, the Elm Trees did not last long as an organization and soon disbanded, its players laying the foundations of other clubs whose teams played match games on Boston Common among themselves and with the senior baseball club, the Olympics.

Among the organized outfits, there existed the following: Tri-Mountain, Green Mountain, Rough and Ready, Hancock, Bay State, Bunker Hill, and Massapoag. Most of these organizations played under the rules adopted by the original Olympic Club. However, paralleling the situation as it developed in the New York area, as more and more matches were played, the equivalent need for uniformity of rules and regulations arose. In 1858, therefore, a call went out among the various clubs for a convention to establish a uniform governing baseball code for New England.

Accordingly, on May 13, 1858, a convention was held in Dedham, Massachusetts, attended by the representatives of ten New England baseball clubs. These delegates framed a constitution and a set of bylaws, as well as a code of playing rules and regulations, all of which were duly adopted by the convention.

Out of this meeting, there also came into being the "Massachusetts Association of Base Ball Players," later called the "New England Association," which organization was the counterpart of the National Association created in New York.

A reading of several rules adopted by the convention will give some idea of the nature of the Massachusetts Game as contrasted to the New York Game.

> RULE 4.—The bases shall be wooden stakes, projecting four feet from the ground.
>
> RULE 8.—The ball must be thrown—not pitched or tossed—to the Bat, on the side preferred by the Striker, and within reach of his Bat.
>
> RULE 14.—If a player, while running the Bases, be hit with the ball thrown by one of the opposite side, before he has touched the home bound, while off a Base, he shall be considered out.
>
> RULE 17.—In playing all match games, one hundred tallies shall constitute the game, the making of which by either Club, that Club shall be judged the winner.
>
> RULE 18.—Not less than ten nor more than fourteen players from each Club, shall constitute a match in all games.

The difference in the basic implement of the game, the ball, should also be noted here: The regulation Massachusetts ball was smaller and about three times lighter in weight than the regulation New York ball*— "not less than two, nor more than two and three-quarter ounces," for the one, as compared to "not less than five and three-fourths nor more than six ounces," for the other.

The first New England club to play according to the New York rules was the Tri-Mountain Base Ball Club of Boston, organized June 16, 1857. The guiding spirit behind this departure from the Massachusetts Game was E. G. Saltzman, who, before moving to New England, had once played second base for the Gotham Club of New York.

The following year, 1858, saw the formation of the second New England club under the New York rules—the Portland Base Ball Club of Portland, Maine.

These two clubs played the first New York-style match ever held in New England, and the game was won by the Portland team, 47 runs to 42. The contest was staged in Massachusetts on the famous Boston Common.

---

* The weight in the New York ball was supplied by the addition of India rubber to the yarn.

It was in a subsequent match (in Portland, Maine, 1859) between these two very clubs, by the way, that the first dive for a base was made by a base runner in New England. The player was Moses E. Chandler of the Tri-Mountain Club, and as James D'Wolf Lovett, a sports writer, later described it, "the feat fairly astonished the natives, who at first roared with laughter; *but Chandler scored the run*, and they then woke up to the fact that a large, new, and valuable 'wrinkle' had been handed out to them."

Although the Massachusetts Game was well entrenched in New England, the advantages—hence the superiority—of the New York Game gradually became known. With this knowledge, fortified by various "trial" games played under the new rules, there came about a reduction in prejudice against the National Association, and many baseball clubs throughout New England decided to play the game under the National banner.

One of the clubs that gave real impetus to the adoption of the New York Game was the prominent Bowdoin Base Ball Club of Boston. The Bowdoins were organized in 1859 with the fullest intention of playing baseball in the traditional Massachusetts manner. However, after giving the new game a trial, they decided to adhere permanently to the National Association rules. That such a club as the Bowdoins had switched its allegiance from the old to the new style of baseball influenced many other clubs; one after another, they also followed suit.

Slowly, the Massachusetts Game gave way to the New York Game, until finally, the National Association of Base Ball Players came into its own. And for the major portion of the next decade, the Association reigned as the sole governing body of baseball in the United States.

As a matter of interest, it may be noted that the first known game of baseball to have been played for a monetary stake was done so under the Massachusetts rules. The game took place at Worcester, Massachusetts, in 1860, between the Unions of Medway and the Excelsiors of Upton. The sum wagered was $1,000, and "100 tallies" were required to win. The game was played over a period of six days, beginning at nine-thirty each morning and halting at five o'clock each afternoon, with a one-hour break in between for lunch.

The journalist who reported the contest, in his final observation, perhaps pinpointed the main reason for the demise of the Massachusetts Game. Said he, "The time occupied in playing the game under such rules was, we think, rather too much of a good thing."

FIVE

◆

BASEBALL
IN THE
CIVIL WAR ERA

During the strife-torn years of the American Civil War, the national pastime passed through a more or less dormant period of growth and development. However, even during the days of bloodshed, when it might be thought that attention could not in good conscience be focused upon such seemingly trivial matters as sporting games, baseball did attract a certain amount of interest—and, for specific matches, even large audiences.

On October 21, 1861, for example, exactly three months after the first battle of Bull Run, over ten thousand people assembled at the Elysian Fields, in Hoboken, to see the so-called "Silver Ball Match" between the picked nines of Brooklyn and New York.

Henry Chadwick, the great sports journalist and baseball historian, arranged the affair, and the New York *Clipper* contributed the prize, a silver ball, from which the match derived its name.

The Brooklyn team, composed of players chosen from the Atlantic, Excelsior, and Eckford baseball clubs, won the match by the score of 18 runs to 6, thereby redeeming the prestige lost to New York in the defeat of 1858.

BASEBALL ON SKATES, WASHINGTON PARK, BROOKLYN

The losing team in 1861 was made up of selected members from five New York clubs: Knickerbocker, Gotham, Empire, Mutual, and Eagle.

The year 1861—incredible as it may sound today—also saw the start of a series of winter baseball games that were played on ice! The first such game, involving teams of players on skates, was a four-inning affair between the Atlantic and Charter Oak Clubs of Brooklyn. An estimated eight to ten thousand spectators witnessed the event, which was won by the Atlantics, 20 runs to 9.

The second game on ice took place two years later, in 1863. And again, a team of the Atlantic club was involved, but this time with a team made up of members of the Star and Charter Oak clubs. Then, right through the ensuing Civil War years and into the following decade, "baseball on ice" continued to be played as a popular winter pastime.

In addition to the above-mentioned organizations, the Empire and Gotham clubs of New York also played the game. And among the various skating areas in which matches were held, there were the following: Washington Skating Pond, Brooklyn; Capitoline Skating Lake, Bedford, Brooklyn; and Sylvan Lake Skating Pond, Hoboken.

It may be observed that just as conventional baseball is subject to the whims of the weather, in a somewhat related way, so, too, were the games on ice. One contest in particular—between the Gotham and Empire clubs at Sylvan Lake, Hoboken—is known to have been halted, on a warm February day in 1864, owing to the unforeseen thawing and breaking up of the actual playing field.

In January 1865, the talented skater-players of the Atlantics defeated the Gothams in a three-game "baseball series on ice," winning two out of the three games played. The scores were: Atlantics 32, Gothams 5; Atlantics 19, Gothams 39; and Atlantics 50, Gothams 30.

Rules of the National Association were used for all contests. However, necessary modifications were made to accommodate the special conditions encountered by playing on ice.

For example, instead of bases, powdered charcoal circles were sprinkled on the "field;" the ball used was soft and nonelastic so as not to wound the players in the crisp, cold air; and a runner was permitted to skate through and beyond a circle (base) only for a distance of five feet. Beyond that distance he was compelled to try for the next circle (base).

THE EXCELSIOR NINE OF 1860

But let it not be forgotten that conventional baseball was being played during the summers of these years as well. James D'Wolf Lovett, writing about it in 1906, described an incident that occurred in Boston during the second year of the Civil War that, in its own way, is reminiscent of one of the most thrilling moments in baseball history—when George Herman "Babe" Ruth, at bat in the third game of the World Series of 1932, pointed to the towering flagpole in center field, then delivered his famous home-run blow beyond it.

On July 10, 1862 (seventy years before Ruth's triumphant moment), the crack Excelsior team of Brooklyn was playing a match game with the prominent Bowdoin team of Boston. It was the first time that a New York club had made a playing trip to the capital of Massachusetts, and according to Lovett, much excitement was created by the visit. He wrote:

> Ball players from all parts of New England came to see them play, and our eyes were opened to many things . . . Much good-natured chaff was passed back and forth between John Lowell and Joe Leggett in this game, which made fun for everybody. Once when the latter was at the bat, he motioned to John, who was then playing centre field, to go back a little further; John backed off about ten feet, upon which Leggett sung out, "A little further, still, John," and the latter, laughing, backed away another ten feet, whereupon Leggett struck a ball and sent it flying over John's head for a home run, amidst shouts of laughter from the crowd.

The Excelsior team, with the famous Jim Creighton pitching for them, won the game by the score of 41 to 15.

Four months earlier, in the Virginia port of Hampton Roads, the Union iron-clad vessel *Monitor*, with a mounted revolving gun turret, had defeated the Confederate vessel *Merrimac*, thereby marking a revolutionary development in naval warfare.

It was the Excelsior club, incidentally, that had made one of the earliest baseball-playing tours ever undertaken in this country. The year was 1860, one year before the start of the Civil War; and the games played during the course of that trip—which took the team through New York State, as well as to the cities of Philadelphia and Baltimore—contributed greatly to the growing popularity of the sport.

But now the nation was torn by strife. Fighting had raged through 1861 and 1862. On January 1, 1863, President Lincoln issued his formal Emancipation Proclamation. In May, an artillery duel was raging across the Rappahannock in Virginia. And, incongruous as it may seem, an old record tells us that as the shells were shrieking, a group of soldiers "entirely heedless" of the battle, "were engaged in a game of base ball just in the rear of the skirmishers."

Years later, no less a personage than Nicholas E. Young, the fourth president of the National League, reminiscing about his Civil War days, wrote:

> In my regiment we had a full cricket team, all of whom had played together at home, and our first match was arranged and played near White Oak Church, Va., in the early spring of 1863, against the Ninety-fifth Pennsylvania Regiment's team, hailing from Philadelphia. About this time (1863) a Base Ball club was organized in the Twenty-seventh New York Regiment, so we turned our attention to Base Ball, and kept it up as we had the chance until the close of the war. It was here that I played my first regular game of Base Ball.

On July 1, 1863, the Battle of Gettysburg began. This was immediately followed by the surrender of Vicksburg to General Grant on Independence Day. By the end of November, the Battle of Chattanooga had opened the road for General Sherman's march through Georgia.

And all through that fateful year, the Eckford Base-Ball Club of Brooklyn had fulfilled its playing commitments without suffering a single defeat on the diamond!* This accomplishment made the Eckfords the acknowledged baseball champions of 1863.

On July 1, 1864, the lead editorial of *The New York Times* began as follows: "There is very little war news of interest this morning. Affairs in front of Petersburgh still remain quiet. There has been no severe fighting now for a week, and the latest dispatches mention that the troops had been relieved somewhat from their sufferings from the heat by cooling showers . . ."

But if, unfortunately, there was "little war news of interest" that morning, there indeed was "interesting" baseball news. On page four of the newspaper, the *Times* informed its readers that heavy showers (perhaps the same showers that had relieved the sufferings of the troops) had put a halt to the championship game between the Atlantic and Empire clubs after the completion of five innings of play. The score at the end of that period stood tied at thirteen runs apiece. The contest had taken place at the Capitoline Ball Grounds, at Bedford, Long Island, with Mr. Yates, of the Eagle Club, officiating as umpire. And viewing the game,

---

* Although the Eckfords played only nine match games in 1863, their undefeated status was no less remarkable since baseball clubs at the time usually played no more than ten or twelve matches each per season. In addition, the Eckfords' record included victories in the many unofficial first-nine, second-nine, and amateur matches played that year.

there had been "at least four thousand spectators, including a large number of ladies."

Three weeks later, on July 22, General Sherman's forces defeated the Confederate troops of General John B. Hood on the battlefields of Georgia.

But war or no war, on the various sporting fields, the baseball season was now in full swing. On the day before the Battle of Atlanta, *The New York Times* printed the following:

BASE BALL.

Atlantic vs. Eagle—Grand Gala Day at Hoboken.

Yesterday afternoon the famous Atlantic Club of Brooklyn, and the Eagle Club of New York, played a game at Elysian Fields, Hoboken, which ended in a victory of the champion Atlantics, by the following score:

Innings.

	1st	2nd	3rd	4th	5th	6th	7th	8th	9th		
Atlantic	3	3	0	8	5	7	7	8	4	—	45
Eagle	0	4	0	0	0	3	0	3	2	—	12

Umpire—Mr. Forsyth, of the Gotham Club.

Mutual vs. Empire.

These celebrated clubs played again yesterday at Hoboken, the result proving as follows, after some most excellent play on both sides:

	1st	2nd	3rd	4th	5th	6th	7th	8th	9th		
Mutual	4	1	3	2	2	2	0	7	3	—	24
Empire	1	0	1	4	2	1	1	1	1	—	12

Umpire—Mr. Grum, of the Eckford Club.

The news dispatch was completed by just two additional sentences that, undoubtedly, were clearly understood by their readers at the time. Today, however, some explanation is probably required. The sentences read as follows: "This afternoon the 'muffin' match between the Mutuals will take place at Elysian Fields, Hoboken, when some jolly fun may be expected. The celebrated billiard *artistes*, Dudley Kavanagh and Wm Goldthwaite, will select sides."

The question today naturally arises: "What in the world is a 'muffin' match?"

The best answer, perhaps, is the definition found in *Beadle's Dime Centennial Base-Ball Player*, a baseball guidebook published in 1876 and edited by Henry Chadwick:

> *Muffins.*—This is a term applied to the poorest class of fielders. A player may be able to hit long balls, and to make home runs, and yet for all that be a veritable muffin, from the simple fact that he can not field, catch, or throw a ball decently. Muffins are the lowest in the class of club nines. Next to them comes the "amateurs," then "second nines," and then "first nines."

A more humorous and "learned" answer, however, may be the one provided by a report made in 1866 by a "committee-of-one" to a society of muffin players in Waterbury, Connecticut. The document reads as follows:

> Your committee to whom was referred the inquiry as to the origin and definition of the word "muffin" beg leave to report: That from a careful examination I find the *origin* somewhat obscure; but am satisfied it had a very early origin, from the fact that I find it compounded with the word "rag" as far back as the Crusades, when the appellation was esteemed highly honorable, indicating valor, virtue and perseverance; indeed, virtue has often been found *clothed in rags.*
>
> The *definition* of the word is less obscure, although some of the modest lexicographers have given it a very simple definition as "a *spongy* cake"; but it is evident that the error has arisen from a lack of knowledge of our illustrious order.
>
> The word Muffin is derived from the Latin *Muggins,* the French *Mufti* (high priest), and the German *Bummi,* and is a clear compound of *Muff* and *fin.* These words are then conjointly conjoined from their close proximity, indicating, among other things, comfort and grace, two conditions closely allied to our order. There are several other words I find belonging to the family, e.g., *puffing,* and *bumming,* and into the latter of these the Muffin generally merges . . .

Now that both origin and definition of the term are clearly understood, it may be stated that "muffin" matches, in addition to regular games, were quite a common occurrence on baseball diamonds throughout the sixties and seventies of the last century. In a sense, they were probably even

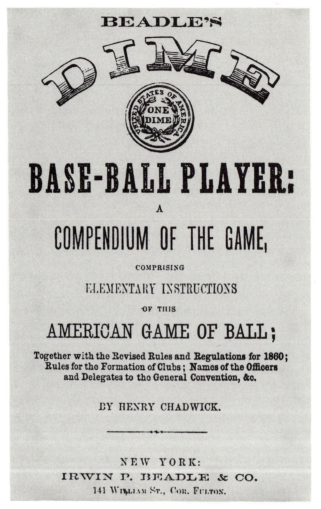

BEADLE'S

DIME

ONE DIME

BASE-BALL PLAYER:

A

COMPENDIUM OF THE GAME,

COMPRISING

ELEMENTARY INSTRUCTIONS

OF THIS

AMERICAN GAME OF BALL;

Together with the Revised Rules and Regulations for 1860;
Rules for the Formation of Clubs; Names of the Officers
and Delegates to the General Convention, &c.

BY HENRY CHADWICK.

NEW YORK:
IRWIN P. BEADLE & CO.
141 WILLIAM ST., COR. FULTON.

Cover of the 1860 edition. In the "Introductory," the following claim is made:
"In presenting this work to our readers, we claim for it the merit of being the
first publication of its kind yet issued."

more popular than the conventional matches; certainly, they were more
diverting to the spectators. And being keenly aware of this, newspaper
editors frequently gave special coverage to such events.

Some idea of how items of this sort were handled by the press may be
obtained from the following brief account (printed in the Washington
Star in 1866) of a match played in the nation's capital between baseball
muffins of the Excelsior and National clubs.

Of the play on the occasion, we have especially to comment on the masterly exhibition of third-base playing by the noted tenor singer, Mr. Lingard (of the Excelsiors). We regret to state, however, that in the fourth inning he had to succumb to the pressure of a ball in the pit of the stomach, which doubled him up and caused him to retire from the field rather sick of the game. One of the Nationals, too, becoming lame, was carried to his bases on a wheelbarrow, but, in trying to make a home-run on wheels, was unmercifully put out at third base . . . Daniell's style of attending to the duties of right-fielding was decidedly unique. He took a seat on the grass, under an umbrella, and leisurely smoked a cigar.

How much "jolly fun" was had at the "muffin" match announced by *The New York Times* on July 21, 1864, however, is a matter of no concern today. Suffice it to say that even as the bloody Civil War was raging, regular baseball, "muffin" matches, and baseball games on ice were being played in various parts of the country.

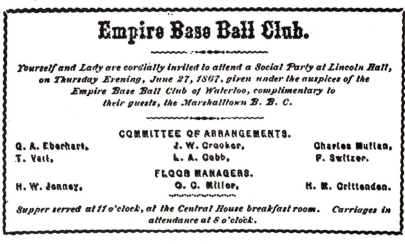

Empire Base Ball Club invitation.

Indeed, often at the direst and most serious moments of life, it is in the nature of human beings to seek diversion and relief by whatever means available. Some escape through sport; others find different amusement.

In the summer of 1864, for instance, as an alternative to baseball, adults in New York, by paying an admission fee of twenty-five cents—children under ten, fifteen cents—were able to visit the remarkable "American Museum" of the fabulous showman, P. T. Barnum.

There, among various other wonders of the world "to be seen at all hours," one could gape at, and be diverted by, the following:

MARVELOUS LIVING AFRICAN MUDFISH, Brought Here in Dry, Solid Clay!! / FOUR SPLENDID SEALS, Just Captured / FAT CHILD, GIANT GIRL, FRENCH GIANT / THE TWO SMALLEST DWARFS LIVING / THE THREE ALBINO CHILDREN / BEAUTIFUL AQUARIA / TWO LIVING KANGAROOS / LIVING PORCUPINE / MINIATURE SKATING POND / MOVING WAX FIGURES / HOUDIN'S AUTOMATON WRITER / THE MUSICAL SEAL / MONSTER SERPENTS and Other Curiosities

All this, while being relieved of the summer's heat by "Nason's new patent ventilator, driven by steam . . . driving and diffusing through the Lecture Room and Museum 30,000 feet of Pure Cool Air Per Minute!"

In the fall, even as decisive battles were being fought, one could often go to the theater to escape the worries of the war. And in the nation's capital, the President of the United States, along with many other individuals, was in the habit of seeking precisely that form of distraction.

HENRY CHADWICK, THE FATHER OF BASEBALL . . .
NESTOR OF AMERICAN SPORT.
From *Sunday Courier*, July, 1907.

Henry Chadwick, the contemporary dean of baseball journalists, happened to be in Washington on one such occasion when the President had gone to the theater. In some correspondence dated November 19, 1864, he described the experience as follows:

It has rained here steadily for the past two days, and you may be assured the attractiveness of the place has not thereby been increased. I visited Grover's new theatre the other night to see Davenport and Wallack in Hamlet. It was the night the President occupied a private box, accompanied by Major-General Hunter and his wife. Mr. Lincoln was evidently an interested and attentive spectator of the performance throughout, as he sat leaning his arm on the edge of the box with his chin on his hand in true Western style. I must confess I was not taken by the appearance of his profile while viewing him in this position. Though he gave an attentive ear to the play, it was not till the grave digger's scene in the fourth act was presented that his particular fancy seemed to have been struck by the occurrences of the drama. You may probably have seen that caricature that Strong of New York used during the late presidential campaign, in which McClellan is represented as Hamlet with Lincoln's head in his hand in the place of Yorick's skull, an Irishman being the grave digger, and Seymour, Horatio. McClellan is made to remark: "I knew him, Horatio, a fellow of infinite jest; where be now your jibes?" From the manner in which Mr. Lincoln enjoyed this whole scene, it was manifest to me he had seen this witty publication; certainly there were others in the house who had. It is well that the occupant of the White House possesses this mental safety valve of humor, or otherwise the immense weight of cares incident to his position must have long since caused him to succumb to the great pressure . . .

Being a sports journalist, Henry Chadwick, in his writings, concerned himself primarily with sporting matters—with baseball and cricket, in particular. However, in his brief vignette of President Lincoln, written by a baseball historian, he has left behind an interesting sidelight on a man touched by Destiny.

But the theater was not the only form of diversion sought by the President during those momentous war years. He also played ball!

In a work entitled *"Abe" Lincoln's Yarns and Stories,* published by The John C. Winston Company of Chicago in 1904, Frank P. Blair relates the following:

During the war my grandfather, Francis P. Blair, Sr., lived at Silver Springs [Maryland], north of Washington, seven miles from the White House. It was a magnificent place of four or five hundred acres, with an extensive lawn in the rear of the house. The grandchildren gathered there frequently. There were eight or ten of us, our ages ranging from eight to twelve years. Although I was but seven or eight years of age, Mr. Lincoln's visits were of such importance to us boys as to leave a clear impression on my memory. He drove out to the place quite frequently. We boys, for hours at a time, played "town ball" on the vast lawn, and Mr. Lincoln would join ardently in the sport. I remember vividly how he ran with the children; how long were his strides, and how far his coat-tails stuck out behind, and how we tried to hit him with the ball, as he ran the bases. He entered into the spirit of the play as completely as any of us, and we invariably hailed his coming with delight.

Lincoln playing ball.

In the 1830s, it will be recalled, it required "sand" for a grown man to play "such childish sports." By the 1860s, no less a man than Abraham Lincoln was running the bases with delight.

Baseball advertisement, 1869

SIX

BASEBALL
AFTER THE REBELLION

One of the important consequences of the Civil War, as far as baseball was concerned, was that the nominally national pastime, in practice, became geographically national as well—at least to a larger degree than before. The many baseball games played by Northern soldiers in Southern prison yards, camp fields, and other areas of the South—witnessed by Southern soldiers and civilians alike—led to the adoption of the sport by Southerners who hitherto had not been familiar with the game.

With the cessation of hostilities, there came about the almost immediate organization of one Southern baseball club after another. In the early spring of 1866, less than a year after peace had been restored, students were playing the game at the University of Virginia; the Monticello Club of Charlottesville had been formed; and baseball clubs were being organized in Washington, Richmond, Staunton, and various other Southern communities.

In fact, a wry observation commonly heard in the North on the way the national game had taken root "down South" was, "It is about the only *national* thing that has!"

The effect on baseball of the Civil War may be measured by still another gauge—the attendance records of the clubs at the annual conven-

THE OFFICERS OF THE NATIONAL ASSOCIATION OF BASE BALL PLAYERS.
From the *Illustrated News*, July 21, 1866.

tions of the National Association of Base Ball Players. From 1859 through 1860, for example, the two years immediately preceding the conflict, the number of clubs represented annually showed a marked increase in attendance. From 1861 through 1864, the war years, club attendance showed a substantial decrease. And in 1865 and 1866, the first two postwar years, club attendance showed a dramatic upsurge. The figures are given below:

PREWAR YEARS	WAR YEARS	POSTWAR YEARS
1859—49 clubs	1861—34 clubs	1865— 91 clubs
1860—62 clubs	1862—32 clubs	1866—202 clubs
	1863—28 clubs	
	1864—30 clubs	

BASEBALL GAME, 1866.
Note how the men and women are separated, the men in the open,
the women under the shelter in the distance.

A state-by-state breakdown of the 1866 attendance records for the tenth annual convention of the National Association of Base Ball Players, which was held at Clinton Hall, New York, shows the following geographical distribution of clubs:

STATE	CLUBS	STATE	CLUBS
New York	73	Tennessee	2
Pennsylvania	48	Missouri	2
New Jersey	26	Kansas	2
Connecticut	20	Delaware	1
Washington, D.C.	10	Virginia	1
Maryland	5	West Virginia	1
Ohio	4	Kentucky	1
Massachusetts	2	Oregon	1
Iowa	2	Maine	1

Aside from all this, the essential fact was that in 1866 the war was definitely over, and baseball was being played. So, in July, the National Club of Washington traveled North to play a return match with the Excelsior Club of Brooklyn, whose team had visited Washington earlier in the year to play the Nationals. *The Union*, a Northern publication, recorded the event as follows:

NATIONAL vs. EXCELSIOR.—Never before in the annals of base ball was there such a reception given a visiting club by another as was accorded to the Nationals by the Excelsiors on July 5th, 1866. In liberal hospitality, in the courtesies extended, and in the truly *recherché* character of the several entertainments provided, together with the munificence of the outlays incurred, the reception will rank among the most noteworthy events in the history of our national game . . . But there were peculiar circumstances connected with the visit of the National Club on this occasion which made it one very appropriate for such a display of kindly courtesy and generous hospitality, inasmuch as the Nationals came here as the representatives of the Southern portion of the base ball fraternity, and as such it was desirable that their brethren of the North should show them that now that peace dwells in our land the sword and musket which, in 1861, were so patriotically grasped by many a member of the fraternity of the North to defend the flag and the life of the nation, are thrown aside, and once more those emblems of more fraternal conflicts—the bat and ball—were taken in hand, and with them all the friendly feelings and forgetfulness of past strife, and also that the animosities of the civil war and the sectional ill-will it developed were discarded with the sword and the rifle, and "with enmity to none and charity for all" our base ball players extended to their brethren of the South the hand of social friendship and fraternal regard, *their* reconstruction policy being that founded on the principle of "Do unto others as you would be done by" . . . the Excelsior

Club of Brooklyn . . . have, by their action in this matter, done more for the restoration of the era of good feeling between the two sections of the country in one day than all our politicians have achieved since the war of the Rebellion terminated.

Of course, despite the highly eloquent sentiments expressed, "the animosities of the civil war and the sectional ill-will it developed" were not so easily "discarded with the sword and the rifle." The time was much too soon after the South's defeat, and the wounds were still quite raw.

A letter from "A True Southerner," printed in *The Union* shortly after the dispatch above appeared, bears this out. The letter read as follows:

Washington, D.C., July 18, 1866.

To the Editor of The Union:
      I hope you will pardon the liberty I take in addressing this note to you, my object being to correct a false impression that might prevail among your readers, if the statements as published in connection with the late visit to New York of the National Base Ball Club of Washington were to remain uncontradicted. Your report, in referring to the reception accorded this Club, alludes to them as "Southerners" . . . Now while I hold no personal animosity to any man or set of men, yet it is an undisputable fact that there is not a single member of the National Club who has any claim to the *proud title of "Southerner;"* on the contrary, nearly every one of them having come from the North during the late *Abolition war,* and the majority of them having served in *that army of mercenaries which invaded the South,* and which *by brute force succeeded in crushing out its liberties.* Knowing this to be their record, I am unwilling that they should be awarded any honors, or receive any encomiums under color of their supposed or assumed Southern character.
      I am, indeed, much surprised that they have not taken measures to correct this impression, but considering their antecedents it was perhaps hardly to be expected.
      Allow me to add that the Potomac Base Ball Club of this city is the only organization of the kind in this vicinity that can really claim the *honor (!)* of being called a "Southern" club, or of *representing Southern sentiment.*
      Again apologizing for trespassing upon your columns, I remain, yours, truly,

A *True Southerner.*

But if sectional animosity prevailed, as indeed it did, the growing common interest in baseball, of both North and South, served in some measure to bind the nation closer together again.

Baseball, in fact, was becoming a dynamic force for curing a host of other moral and physical evils as well.

In Philadelphia, a group of churchmen took up the sport and played the game at regular intervals. And in Brooklyn, the Reverend C. H. Everest, pastor of the Puritan Congregational Church, alluded to the game from the pulpit.

Baseball, said the pastor, is a game "whose regulations are calculated to prevent the ill feelings engendered by other games; and one, moreover, which serves to attract our young men from places of bad repute, and to supply the right kind of exercise and amusement."

Referring to his fellow churchmen in the Quaker City, he continued, "This opinion has been practically endorsed by several clergymen of Philadelphia who last year formed themselves into a base ball club for purposes of healthful and moral recreation, in imitation of the hundreds of English parsons who take such delight in playing cricket on the commons of their villages."

As a direct result of the clergymen's baseball activities, the Reverend Everest said, "their sermons are stronger and more attractive, their physical ability greater, and their intellects clearer and brighter for the relaxation from their arduous cares and trying duties."

The remarkable powers attributed to baseball did not stop there, however. In the spring of 1866, for example, it was feared that an epidemic of cholera would strike the nation in the wake of the Civil War and on the heels of a lingering winter. Newspapers and journals, as a consequence, were filled with notices and advertisements for specifics, remedies, and various patent preventives against the disease. Then, lo and behold, baseball began to be touted as perhaps the most effective agent of all against cholera! Articles appeared stressing the inherent health benefits in the game and how, by indulging in the sport, it was possible to combat the epidemic disease.

This, for instance, is what *The Daily News* (in much the same words used by another contemporary newspaper, the *Mercury*) said upon the subject:

> There is but one fact connected with this manly exercise and healthful out-door recreation which specially commends it to popularity

this season, in view of the approaching epidemic of cholera; and that is, that no sanitary measure that can be adopted—in addition to that of temperance and cleanliness—is so calculated to induce that healthy condition of the system which acts as a barrier to the progress of this disease as base ball exercise every afternoon. The free perspiration induced; the active circulation of the blood to the surface of the body, consequent upon the healthy action of the skin; the vitality and strength derived from a constant inhalation of pure oxygen of the atmosphere of the ball fields, together with the vigor imparted generally by open air exercise in which every muscle of the body is brought into play, are all conducive to a high degree of health . . . hence all who can spare the time, for their health's sake alone, should join some ball club this Summer and take an active part in the exercises of the field every fine afternoon. This will be found a specific against cholera far more effective, than any of the drug mixtures so highly commended in certain journals, for it is that which nature points out as the proper course to pursue.

Actually, if the temper of the times is taken into consideration, it is not too surprising that articles of this type were published. For most newspapers and periodicals of the era frequently did carry such material, in addition to medical and pharmaceutical advertisements that today not only would be illegal, but, if they did find their way into print, would also immediately be characterized as quack or fraudulent.

An example, which appeared repeatedly in such a reputable newspaper as *The New York Times*, is the following:

Cancer. Tumor. Scrofula.

A speedy and permanent cure. Dr. Joseph T. Robinson has discovered an infallible remedy for the cure of cancer, tumor and scrofula. Has sufficient testimony to convince the most incredulous of his entire success in this branch of practice. Terms are no cure no pay, which should enlist public confidence.

Office hours, 10 to 12 A.M. and 2 to 4 P.M.

Joseph T. Robinson.

No. 461 Broome-st.—a few doors west of Broadway.

Compared to the "cancer-cure" ad, the article on baseball and cholera was relatively harmless; for if baseball was not in fact a certified anticholera specific, the game truly did provide a form of healthful outdoor exercise, which conceivably could strengthen resistance against disease.

Pursuing this line of thinking, *The City Item* of Philadelphia, in August of 1866, said:

> The increase of strength from playing base ball is providing many of our weak young men with strong chests and tall, robust, muscular figures. It well deserves the name of "Our National Game," as it is played everywhere, and has benefits manifold. How much happier are the mothers and the fathers, whose children instead of playing in the streets, and in imminent danger of being run over by some blockhead of a drayman, are found on the ball field, enjoying themselves in this fine recreation. How quickly their fears of safety vanish, how delightedly they sit by their attentive son as he describes the game, and listen to his eloquent remarks of satisfaction and happiness. What a blessing is conveyed by those two words, base ball.

But if some were finding baseball "a blessing," others were dismayed by the discovery that the pastime was becoming a business. For some years, rumors had been circulating that individual baseball clubs (all of which were amateur) had been secretly paying certain of their star players to keep them on their rosters. Payments were reputed to consist of outright salaries, bonuses, jobs, gifts, and various other forms of compensation. The youthful pitching wizard Jim Creighton, of the Brooklyn Excelsiors, was even said to have received some kind of salary from the club years before he died, in 1861, at the tender age of twenty-one.

But now, in 1866, it was openly being stated that the Athletic Base Ball Club of Philadelphia had engaged the services of four "professional" baseball players. Rumors had given way to undisguised accusations, and this was a very serious matter, since—as it will be recalled—club baseball was regarded as strictly an outdoor game, played by gentlemen for exercise —consequently, a sport of amateurs.

The reputed action of the Philadelphia Club, therefore, put the city on the spot, so to speak, in gentlemanly sporting circles; and comment was more or less unrestrained.

In a column labeled "Special Correspondence," *The City Item* of Philadelphia published a communication that read as follows:

> New York, August 7, 1866.—*Dear Item:*—I must confess that the idea of a club like the Athletic, of your city, having "paid" players, absolutely startled the base ball fraternity in this city, when they heard about it. Such a sensation was never before created, and when it was discovered that men from this vicinity were the recipients of

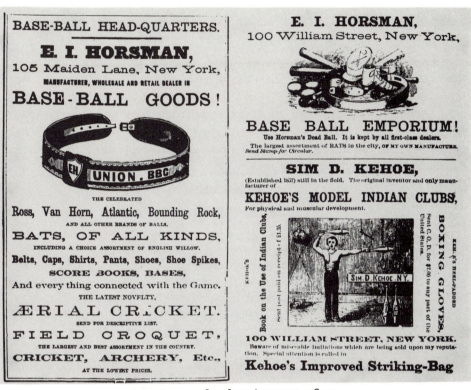

Sporting goods advertisement, 1870

the pay, universal indignation was felt and expressed . . . The "paying system" has never been tried here, and would, without doubt, if attempted, meet an early death . . . What must be the contempt for those who would degrade our great "National Game," and make it a *business*. When such becomes the case, farewell to base ball; the excitement, which is, at present, attendant on these contests, will cease, then the game itself will gradually, but surely, die out . . .

Additional pressure was brought to bear on the Philadelphia baseball club by the newspaper itself, which printed the following in its editorial column:

It begins to look as if the Athletics would soon dispense with the services of their four hired men. Off with their heads! . . . The New York papers are full of flings at Philadelphia on account of our "hired men" . . . Shall we play ball as gentlemen, or shall we hire men to win? . . . The Athletic Club will retrieve itself yet. The

gentlemen in the club will compel the officers to do the fair thing . . .
The year of jubilee has come—return ye ransomed sinners home!

However, if the publishers of *The City Item* were concerned about
the ethics involved in making baseball a "business," they certainly were
not averse to using the popularity of the sport to advance their own business interests. For at about the very same time they were decrying the
Athletics' alleged action of paying players who conceivably could help
them win ball games, the newspaper's owners were appealing in advertisements to baseball clubs as follows:

Splendid Offer!

To close August 31, 1866.

Encouraged by the success which attended their recent offers to
Base Ball Clubs, the Proprietors of the *Philadelphia City Item* are
induced to offer additional inducements, as follows:—

The Club sending us the largest list of subscribers by August
31, shall receive the First Premium, as follows:—1 dozen Horsman's
celebrated regulation Balls, a complete set of Horsman's Improved
Bases, 12 Caps, made to order, 1 dozen best Bats. The First Premium worth in all, say $50.

Second Premium, for Second largest list—1 dozen Horsman's
celebrated regulation Base Balls, and 1 dozen best Bats.

Third Premium, for Third largest list—1 dozen Horsman's celebrated Balls.

Fourth Premium—Beautiful Score Book.

The Clubs competing will receive one copy of *The City Item*
for one year for every $3 sent.

*Every Club sending ten subscribers, ($3 each,) shall receive
one dozen Horsman's best Balls.*

Now, gentlemen, let us see what you can do. Begin at once!

Fitzgerald & Co.,
114 South Third street, Philadelphia.

In other words, so far as *The City Item* was concerned, sport should
remain sport, but the newspaper business—well, that was another matter.
If the amateur baseball clubs could help build up newspaper circulation
simply by engaging in a harmless little commercial competition for equipment premiums, why, another yardstick could be applied for measuring
gentlemen's "sporting" activities.

Realistically viewed, however, the furor in Philadelphia was simply an outgrowth of developing conditions everywhere. Baseball suddenly had become a great and popular spectator sport, and many thousands of people were flocking to the various ball grounds to watch their favorite teams play. As the audiences grew, so grew the intensity of competition. Club rivalries became sharper and more clearly defined. By 1867, for instance, any team that was able to defeat the crackerjack Atlantics of Brooklyn in two games out of three felt it had earned the right to tag the word "champions" to its name. Indeed, by virtue of such achievement, the players of the Union Base Ball Club of Morrisania that year called themselves "Champions of the United States." The drive to win games, rather than the desire to indulge in friendly "exercise," had now become the motivating force behind the sport.

The inevitable result was that in order to secure the best playing talent available, clubs began to compete with one another *off*, as well as on, the playing field. And if such talent could be attracted by the simple expedient of making discreet payments to good players as inducements to join or stick with the club, then that was what was done. For a winning baseball club suddenly had become a matter of civic pride and prestige, and the realization had dawned on the commercial segment of the community that large crowds attending baseball games were also good for business: People *bought* things; they ate, drank, used hotels, needed transportation, required services, spent money for entertainments, etc.

In short, baseball now was very much, and very closely, connected with business. Indeed, it *was* a business. For as the crowds grew larger and larger, the owners of the various ball grounds, one after another, began to enclose the playing fields and charge admission to witness games.

In the earlier days, the diamond was laid out on an open meadow, while spectators sat or stood about on the fringes of the field. Then, in 1862, William Cammeyer, the enterprising owner of the Union Club's baseball grounds in Brooklyn, conceived the idea of enclosing the field and charging an admission fee of ten cents for the privilege of seeing a game. Cammeyer allowed the club free use of the grounds, and he, in turn, pocketed the admission receipts. This arrangement prevailed for one year; then the Unions realized the money potential involved in the situation and refused to play unless gate receipts were shared. Cammeyer bowed to the demand, and the club was "in business."

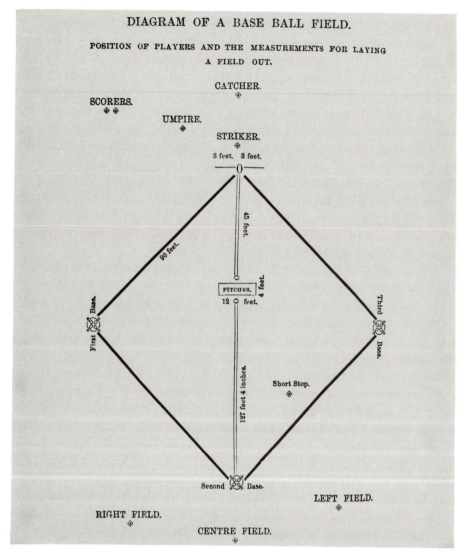

DIAGRAM OF A BASE BALL FIELD.

POSITION OF PLAYERS AND THE MEASUREMENTS FOR LAYING A FIELD OUT.

1866 dimensions. The layout is about the same today, except that the distance between the pitcher and batter has been increased about 15 feet.

As more and more baseball fields were enclosed, and as the practice of "gate-sharing" spread, many clubs discovered that they were thus enabled to cover their operating expenses and, in some cases, even wind up the season with a handsome profit.

The Standard

"TRUTH WITHOUT FEAR."

Saturday, April 19th, 1869,

BASE BALL.

THE NEW CLUB AND NEW BALL GROUNDS. —The lots situated on the corner of Lee ave. and Rutledge street, occupied last winter by the Union Skating Association, have been enlarged, levelled and laid out into ball grounds, with ground room enough to accommodate three clubs. Houses and benches, &c, will be erected, and everything to make the grounds complete will be done by the enterprizing President, Mr. Cammeyer.

Which three clubs will occupy these grounds has not yet been settled, and none, we believe, have made application except the Rutledge Club. An admission fee of 10 cents will be charged on *match* days. These grounds, if managed properly—and there is little doubt but that they will be—could be made not only to prove very profitable, but a credit to the section in which they are located. They are conveniently situated, and accessible to both districts—the Flushing, Division avenue and Greenpoint cars running within a few blocks of the grounds.

Progress report on the construction of the Union baseball grounds in Brooklyn. Also, the announcement that a ten-cent admission fee would be charged to all match games.

The conclusion, therefore, became inescapable! *There was money to be made in baseball!*

Before long, this single fact loomed large on the financial horizon; for, on the heels of the latter discovery, the more important baseball clubs incorporated themselves as "business" companies, issued stock, and found themselves right in the center of clever investment deals and speculation. This situation prevailed through the early seventies, by which time baseball, curiously, had become as common a subject of conversation in the stock market as in sporting circles. In addition, newspapers, which hitherto had devoted space to the subject only in their sports columns, now felt compelled to cover the game on their financial page as well. Typical is the following excerpt from the *New York Clipper,* a contemporary publication:

THE BASE BALL STOCK MARKET

The fluctuations in fancy stocks last week equals the ups and downs of the gold market in panic times. Last week we quoted Atlantic as high as 115, and afterwards 112; on Saturday it touched 107, with a downward tendency . . . Excelsior has gone up to par, and holders are expecting a further rise . . . Eureka stock is on the list again—Newark purchasers taking it at 96½ . . . Mutual fell off considerably at Saturday's Board—it being sold as low as 96. The market is very feverish at present, the speculative operators being very lively.

If the above appears odd and somewhat out of place in connection with baseball, consider the following, which appeared on May 14, 1963, about a century later, in the financial pages of *The New York Times.*

BALL CLUB SCORES ON WALL ST.

The San Francisco Giants baseball team, now leading the National League, is scoring in Wall Street.

In the over-the-counter market yesterday, units of the National Exhibition Company, owner of the Giants, were being quoted at their highest levels of 1963 at 750 bid and 800 offered. On March 22, by contrast, the market was 625 bid and 675 offered . . .

Anheuser-Busch, Inc., better known for its beer than for its baseball interests, owns the St. Louis Cardinals, now in second place behind the Giants. Anheuser-Busch shares edged up ⅛ yesterday to 54⅛ bid and 54⅝ asked. But this market price mainly reflects the brewery business.

Here, then, in the marketplace for stocks and bonds, the traditional realm of high finance, and in the widespread practice of "gate-sharing," was professional baseball truly born. For although many players ultimately did make professional careers out of ball-playing, baseball as a business began not, as is so often claimed, with the piddling payments made in secret to individual players, but with the ball clubs first covering their operating expenses, then with their making of actual money profits.

The game, in the aftermath of the Rebellion, had indeed come a long way from a common children's pastime. Nevertheless, major milestones lay ahead.

SEVEN

THE RISE
OF
PROFESSIONAL BASEBALL

We are a band of Ball Players,
    From "Cincinnati City,"
We go to toss the ball around,
    And sing to you our ditty,
And if you'd listen to the song
    We are about to sing,
We'll tell you all about "base ball,"
    And make the welkin ring.

—Verse one, Club Song of the
Cincinnati "Red Stockings"—1869

Heralding the baseball season of 1867, *The New York Times* said, "There is scarcely a village throughout the country which does not contain one or more associations devoted to the exposition of the beauties of our national game."

Two years later, the same paper reported that by actual number there were over one thousand regularly organized baseball clubs in the United

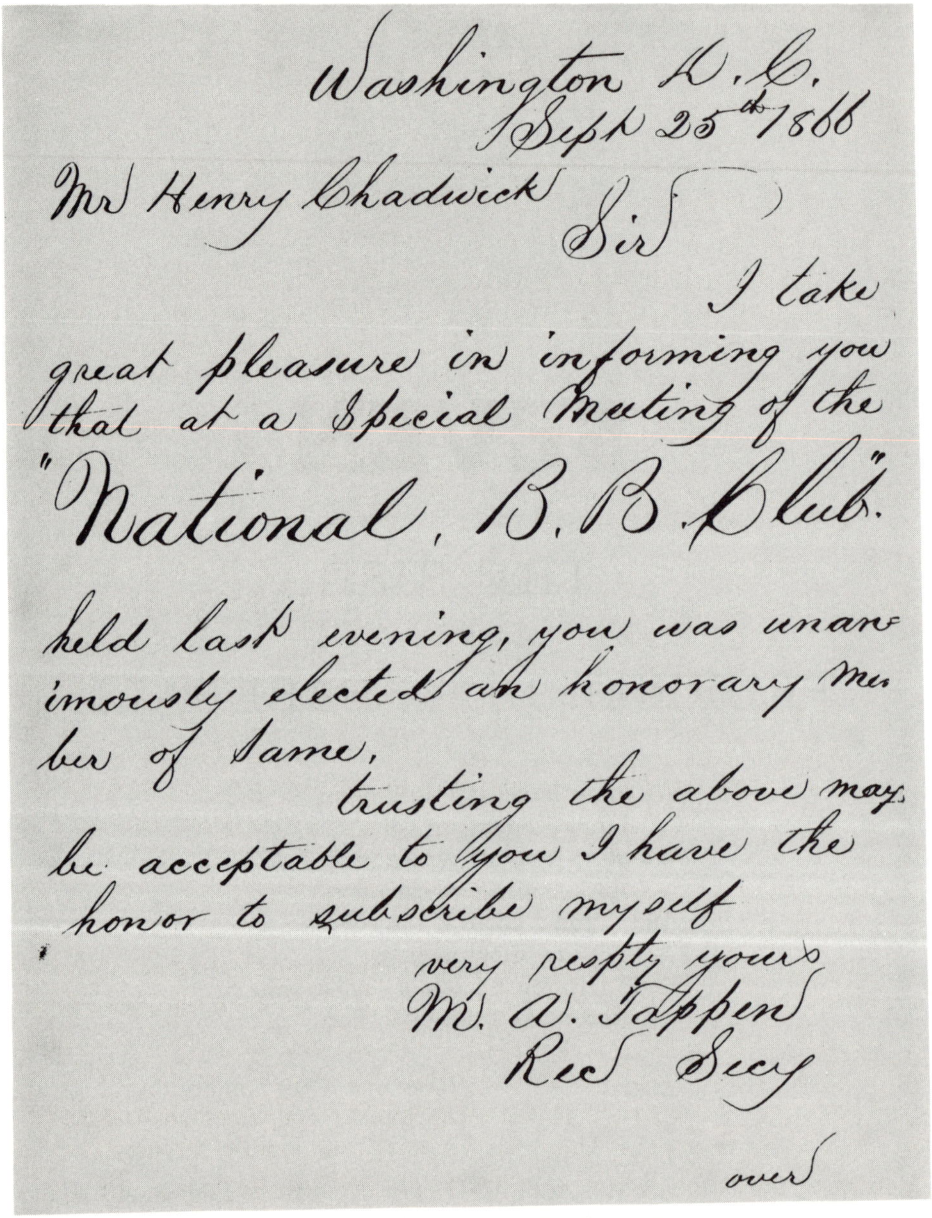

Washington D.C.
Sept 25th 1866

Mr Henry Chadwick
        Sir

           I take
great pleasure in informing you
that at a Special Meeting of the
"National, B.B Club."
held last evening, you was unan-
imously elected an honorary Mem
ber of Same,
        trusting the above may
be acceptable to you I have the
honor to subscribe myself
         very respty yours
         M. A. Tappen
         Rec Secy

                over

Letter to Henry Chadwick informing him that he had been made an honorary member of the National Base Ball Club of Washington on September 24, 1866. The following year, Chadwick accompanied the team as official scorekeeper on the first extended playing tour undertaken by an Eastern club to the West.

States and that over 200,000 persons had "gathered as spectators" at important contests during the preceding season—"as many as 10,000 people at a time."

As an indication of what this meant in terms of dollars and cents, it was said that seven or eight professional organizations had divided "no less than $100,000 in the form of gate-money receipts" during 1868; and one club alone, the Mutuals of New York, had earned profits of $15,000— an enormous sum at the time.

These figures become even more impressive when it is recalled that only ten short years had elapsed since the National Association of Base Ball Players was organized by the representatives of a mere handful of amateur clubs. And, furthermore, those years had included the relatively dormant athletic period of the Civil War.

As has been noted, various factors contributed to the phenomenal growth in popularity of baseball, but one of the most important was the first extended playing tour ever undertaken by an Eastern ball club through the western part of the nation. This tour took place during the season of 1867, when the National Club of Washington, composed mainly of federal government employees (mostly clerks), set out for the West, and played a total of ten games in a number of different cities, which included Columbus, Cincinnati, Indianapolis, Louisville, Chicago, and St. Louis.

Henry Chadwick, acting as official scorekeeper and also as roving correspondent for several Eastern newspapers, accompanied the team on its journey. The reports he sent back—plus the fact that the local press everywhere also covered the contests—gave the tour wide publicity.

The Nationals won nine out of the ten games they played, losing only to the Forest City Base Ball Club, at Dexter Park, Chicago, by the relatively "close" score of 23 to 29.

This loss (on July 25) to the Forest City players, coupled with the subsequent victory of the Nationals over the Excelsior Club of Chicago (on July 26) provided the raw materials for one of the very first controversies—if not the first—in baseball, involving public accusations and charges of sellout, fraud, corruption, and gambling.

The controversy began innocently enough when the Chicago press, with a mixture of local pride and a lack of real baseball knowledge, misinterpreted the defeat of the Nationals by the Forest City Club as presaging an easy victory for the so-called "Champions of the West," the Excelsiors of Chicago. The local papers, in a spirit of braggadocio, all

The Ball Players Chronicle

printed editorials predicting the triumph of Chicago and the demise of the visitors. The *Chicago Times,* for example, stated:

> When the Nationals shall have lived among us a few days, imbibed pure water from the clear depths of Lake Michigan, breathed the healthy breezes from the prairies, and taken a few lessons in base ball playing, they will begin to realize how profitable has been their trip to the Northwest.

What happened, of course, was that the Nationals, reading the Chicago papers, became more determined than ever to win the game on July 26—and they did, before the largest crowd ever assembled to watch a baseball game outside of New York and Philadelphia. As reported, "by 4 P.M. there could not have been less than ten thousand people encircling the players, between five and six hundred occupying carriages, every hack in the city being engaged at an early hour, while not a light wagon was to be had at a livery stable, so great was the demand." Admission was fifty cents, a rather high fee for the times.

What made the Chicago defeat even more ignominious was the lop-sided score by which the Excelsiors lost—49 to 4. For the Nationals, in light of the dire predictions of the Chicago press, the victory was particularly sweet. For the Chicago team, by contrast, the defeat was humiliating.

Then came the newspaper reactions.

Seizing upon the rumors spread by disappointed gamblers—namely, that the Nationals had deliberately "thrown" the game to Forest City so as to set up large bets on the Chicago game—the editorial writers branded the National Club as a group of men "whose trade was base ball, and who looked to the money received for entrance fees, and gained by betting, for the means of subsistence."

"THE CLIPPER GOLD MEDAL."
Awarded in 1868 by *The Clipper*, the famous sporting paper, "one medal for each player in his position, from catcher to right field, who excelled in averages on outs and runs."

The *Tribune* called the affair "a regular confidence game." The *Republican*, more politely, accused the Washington team of "unfair conduct." And the *Times*, in a humorous vein, declared Chicago the real victor—"the greatest muffs in the country."

As might be expected, when the visiting players had finished reading all these articles, their collective feeling was one of outrage—and all the more so because the team was entirely innocent of the charges. There was much talk of libel suits and other actions to be taken, but finally the president and the ex-president of the club, Colonel Frank Jones and Mr. Gorman, respectively, simply stated their position to the editors of the *Chicago Tribune* and the *Chicago Republican* and demanded printed retractions of the newspaper charges.

As a result, and as a conciliatory gesture, the *Tribune* printed an *"amende honorable,"* which appeared in the issue of July 29, 1867; and the *Republican,* on the same day, printed the following letter:

To the Editor of the Chicago Republican:

Sir: As President of the National Club of Washington, D.C., I feel called upon to reply to the foul aspersions upon the character of our club, contained in an editorial of your issue of to-day, headed "The Base Ball Contest."

In doing this, I at once pronounce the statements made false in every particular, as far as they refer to the National Club. It is false that we travel around the country for gambling purposes; it is false that the game with the Rockford Club was "thrown;" it is false that our nine is a "picked nine;" and, lastly, it is false that noted gamblers accompany our club, or that such a class is in any way countenanced by the National Club.

Our defeat on Thursday was as legitimate a one as was our victory yesterday, and as great a surprise to us, and as much of a disappointment as was that of the Excelsiors yesterday to their friends in Chicago. With as much justice might the Excelsior Club be charged with throwing their game yesterday for betting purposes, as we are for our errors of Thursday; the contrast between the fielding of the Excelsiors in the early part of the game of yesterday and their play in the latter innings being as unaccountable as our glaring weakness in the field and at the bat on Thursday.

The boastful editorials in the Chicago papers on Friday had much to do with our victory of yesterday, as they proved a powerful incentive to extra exertions. *A generous, high-toned press should have accorded us due praise for a victory as fairly won as was our previous defeat fairly sustained, but liberal sentiments never go hand in hand with partisan braggadocio and partisan disappointment.*

But for the fact that your statements have been made upon supposed reliable information, I should have taken a different course of action in the matter. As it is, however, I trust this statement will be sufficient to induce a retraction of the gross aspersions upon the reputation of a club which, I think, stands as high in the estimation of the fraternity as any club attached to the National Association . . .

Trusting that in common justice to us you will give this as prominent a place in your columns as was given the editorial remarks referred to, I remain yours, etc.,

Frank Jones,
President National Base Ball Club.

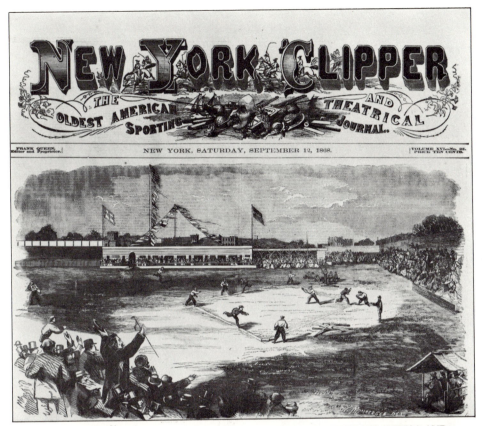

CHAMPIONSHIP BASE BALL MATCH BETWEEN BROOKLYN ATLANTICS AND
PHILADELPHIA ATHLETICS AT UNION GROUNDS, WILLIAMSBURG, L.I.,
SEPTEMBER 7, 1868.

During the ten games played on the tour, the Washington team
ran up a total of 735 runs, against only 175 runs for their opposition. This
was quite an accomplishment, for unlike most Eastern clubs, the Nationals had but one "professional" player on their team, George Wright,
who in later years founded the large sporting-goods business that bore his
name.

Since the club was practically one hundred per cent amateur, the
Nationals did not engage in the prevailing practice of "gate-sharing." The
tour, consequently, cost the team approximately $3,000 in expenses. But
for this sum, and their achievements on the diamond, the club earned
the honor of having played an important role in popularizing the American
national pastime.

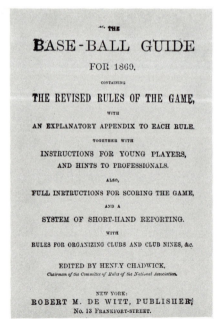

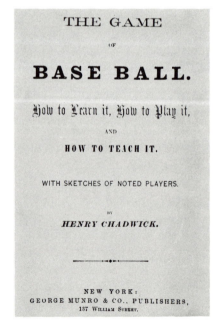

Early baseball guidebooks of the nineteenth century.

In 1868, the National Association repealed the prohibition against professional players participating in match games between Association member clubs. This legislative act, in effect, openly recognized that professionals, to a large extent, had been playing the game; and it came as a late effort by the National body to try to retain control of the rapidly changing "amateur" sport.

The new rule adopted by the Association read as follows: "Rule Fifth—Sec. 7. All players who play base ball for money, or who shall at any time receive compensation for their services as players, shall be considered professional players, and all others shall be regarded as amateur players."

Commenting on the subject at the opening of the subsequent season, *The New York Times* said:

> This amendment to the rules may be regarded as one of the most important ever made . . . Custom will now rank every club as a professional organization which has a majority of its nine composed of professional players. Amateur clubs, however, can employ a professional to take charge of their grounds or to instruct them, but he cannot be played in their nine in a match without the consent of the contesting club, unless they offset the advantage by playing a professional themselves.

Regarding the final effect of the action, however, William Ingraham Harris some years later wrote:

> This was the beginning of the end of the National Association as an amateur body or as a guardian of the baseball interests of the country. Its mission had been fulfilled, and, although its jurisdiction was acknowledged during the next two years, the professionals monopolized the attention of the country, and amateur clubs soon ceased to be of any national importance.

But the time was now 1869; during this year, some of the most noteworthy events in the annals of baseball were to take place; and most of these events, as will be seen, were linked with the exploits of a single club —the fabulous "Red Stockings" of Cincinnati.

To the Red Stockings belongs the distinction of having been the first baseball club known to have been organized on an entirely professional basis. The members of that historic team, positions, and salaries (openly paid), have been recorded as follows:

CINCINNATI "RED STOCKINGS"—1869		
PLAYER	POSITION	SALARY
Harry Wright	Center field	$1,800
George Wright	Short stop	1,800
Asa Brainard	Pitcher	800
Charles Gould	1st base	800
Fred Waterman	3rd base	800
Charles J. Sweasy	2nd base	700
Douglass Allison	Catcher	700
Andrew J. Leonard	Left field	700
Calvin A. McVey	Right field	700
Richard Hurley	Substitute	600
	Total salaries	$9,400.

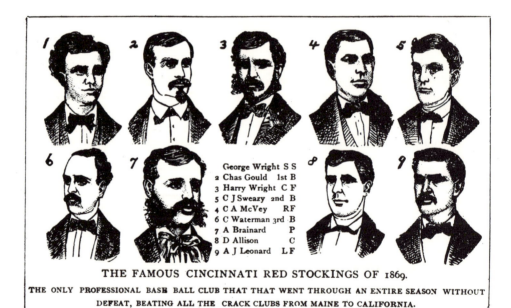

THE FAMOUS CINCINNATI RED STOCKINGS OF 1869.

THE ONLY PROFESSIONAL BASE BALL CLUB THAT THAT WENT THROUGH AN ENTIRE SEASON WITHOUT DEFEAT, BEATING ALL THE CRACK CLUBS FROM MAINE TO CALIFORNIA.

THE FAMOUS CINCINNATI RED STOCKINGS OF 1869

Today, a century later, the total Red Stocking payroll of $9,400 stands in marked contrast to the huge six-figure salaries drawn by certain ballplayers of our time (for example, Ted Williams, Joe DiMaggio, Stan

THE PICKED NINE OF THE "RED STOCKING" BASEBALL CLUB, CINCINNATI, OHIO.
Hurley, Sub.; G. Wright, S.S.; Allison, C.; McVey, R.F.; Leonard, L.F.; Sweasy,
2nd B.; Waterman, 3rd B.; H. Wright, C.F.; Brainard, P.; Gould, 1st B.
From *Harper's Weekly*, July 3, 1869.

Musial, Willie Mays, Sandy Koufax, Mickey Mantle, and others), each of whom has received at least $100,000 for a single season's effort.

But beyond the fact that Cincinnati was the pioneer professional club of the nation, what really makes the team memorable is another more striking phenomenon—its incredible record of victories during its first year of wholly professional play.

During 1869, the Cincinnati players toured the country from coast to coast, and by the time the season ended, both the name of the team and the city it hailed from were common household words. For, unbelievably, the Red Stockings emerged the victorious, undefeated, baseball champions of the United States!

A colorful nineteenth-century account described aspects of the tour as follows:

Cincinnati Base Ball Club.

SCHEDULE OF

Games on Eastern Trip.

JUNE, 1869.

No. Game.	Month.			
1	May	31	Monday.....	ANTIOCH, Yellow Springs.
2	June	1	Tuesday	INDEPENDENT, Mansfield.
3	"	2	Wednesday	FOREST CITY, Cleveland.
4	"	3	Thursday..........	NIAGARA, Buffalo.
5	"	4	Friday..............	ALERT, Rochester.
6	"	5	Saturday	CENTRAL CITY, Syracuse.
	"	6	Sunday	Albany.
7	"	7	Monday...........	UNION, Lansingburg.
8	"	8	Tuesday...........	NATIONAL, Albany.
	"	9	Wednesday	
9	"	10	Thursday.........	LOWELL, Boston.
10	"	11	Friday...........	TRIMOUNTAIN, Boston.
11	"	12	Saturday	HARVARD, "
	"	13	Sunday	New Haven.
12	"	14	Monday...........	YALE, "
13	"	15	Tuesday...........	ECKFORD, Brooklyn.
14	"	16	Wednesday........	ATLANTIC, "
15	"	17	Thursday.........	MUTUAL, New York.
	"	18	Friday...........	
16	"	19	Saturday	OLYMPIC, Philadelphia.
	"	20	Sunday...........	"
17	"	21	Monday	ATHLETIC, "
18	"	22	Tuesday	KEYSTONE, "
	"	23	Wednesday	
19	"	24	Thursday	MARYLAND, Baltimore.
20	"	25	Friday...........	NATIONAL, Washington.
21	"	26	Saturday..........	OLYMPIC, "
	"	27	Sunday......	"
22	"	28	Monday...........	OLYMPIC, "
	"	29	Tuesday...........	
23	"	30	Wednesday	BALTIC, Wheeling.
	July	1	Home...	

Cincinnati schedule of 1869

Monday morning early the start was made . . . No bands, no enthusiasm, no send off. Tickets were in hand, but only $24 in money remained. Some members of the nine, forgetful of pledges, had touched the rosy [liquor] too freely. All were cross. And the miraculous task of transporting this insubordinate band a couple of thousand miles on $24 and chance began.

The travelers, as equipped on leaving Cincinnati, had in their possession two dozen bats, one dozen balls, the club pennant, tickets for Boston, $24 in cash and a bottle of arnica. A detailed account of the finances of this trip would look ludicrous. The first game at Yellow Springs was missed, a heavy rain prevailing all morning. At Mansfield the nine got out of town, having just made enough to liquidate the board bill, with a like result at Cleveland, Buffalo and Rochester. They reached Troy penniless and hopeless, but had their hearts gladdened in the afternoon on receiving from the Troy manager $285 as their share of the admission fees. This was all subsequently expended in Boston, where the chief game was played with the Lowells on the Common, and the next with the Harvards, on the well known Jarvis fields. Rain prevented contests with the New Havens and Yales, and the nine landed in New York City, bankrupt for the second time. The next three days, however, yielded $1,700, as follows: $300 from the Mutuals, $600 from the Atlantics and $800 from the Athletics, and the club returned to Cincinnati, having made a clear profit of $1,600. This was the trip which gave the Reds their fame, the home members confidently expecting that when Troy was reached the renowned Haymakers, considered the most powerful team in the East, would administer a dressing to the Cincinnatis—a thing they were not successful in doing. Albany, Springfield, Boston and New York were visited in the order named, at the latter place occurring the great 4–2 game with the Mutuals, then unprecedented in its score . . . The following day the champion Atlantics lowered their colors to the Ohioans, the result being 32 to 10. On Thursday a victory was won over the Eckfords. Success continued in New York, Philadelphia, Baltimore, Washington and Wheeling, arousing Cincinnatians to a fever of excitement, as evinced by the following dispatch:

Cincinnati, June 15, 1869.

Cincinnati B.B.C., Earle's Hotel, N.Y.:

On behalf of the citizens of Cincinnati we send you greeting. The streets are full of people, who give cheer after cheer for their pet club. Go on with the noble work. Our expectations have been met.

All the Citizens of Cincinnati,
Per S.S. Davis.

The nine arrived home on July 1, and the *Commercial* of the following day thus describes its reception: "Cincinnati wore a holiday attire yesterday in honor of the men who have carried her name victorious over everything that dared contest the supremacy. The little Miami depot and the streets to the north were densely crowded yesterday morning by thousands of men, women and children on the arrival of the train bearing the champion nine of the United States. As the train slowly entered the depot, the Zouave band sounded the notes of welcome, and cheer after cheer went up from thousands of lungs. The procession, headed by the band wagon, moved west to Pike, north to Fourth, west to Walnut and north to the Gibson House. Along the line of march throngs lined the sidewalks, the men cheering and the ladies waving their handkerchiefs. On Fourth, from Broadway to Elm, there was a gay sight of flags and banners bearing hearty words of greeting. Many were on the streets who knew nothing of the game, but nevertheless felt a pride in the club. Said an old gentleman and prominent business man, who looked earnestly at the nine as they filed slowly by in open carriages: "I know nothing of base ball, but it does me good to see those young fellows. They've done something to add to the glory of the city." "Glory," said an eager young merchant. "They've advertised the city—advertised us, sir, and helped our business, sir." On arrival at the Gibson House the nine were escorted upstairs to the balcony, in front of the parlors. When they made their appearance on the balcony, cheer after cheer was given, and demands were made for a speech from each of the players. In response to calls, Mr. Champion [President of the club] came forward, and in a few well chosen words thanked the citizens for the interest manifested in the victorious career of the club and for the splendid reception. In conclusion, he stated that the boys were tired with much playing and traveling, and that they all, in consequence, desired to be excused.

A reception game was played in the afternoon, with a picked nine, and on the arrival there of the Red Stockings they were presented with a bat of ash, 27 feet in length, 19½ inches in diameter at the butt, and 9½ inches at the wrist. Handsomely painted on it were the names of the nine. A magnificent banquet was given at the Gibson House that night.

So ended the "March to the Sea." In a few days trips were made to the Northwest, and in September to California. Every game was won and a record made which has never been equaled.

The Bill of Fare used at the "magnificent banquet" has been preserved. From it, we know that the victorious baseball players, who on several occasions during their tour were penniless and hungry, that night dined on such exotic dishes as buffalo tongue, decorated en gelée; Westphalia ham, decorated à la Richelieu; Baron of Veal, ornamented à la jardinière; filet of beef, larded with mushrooms; mountain oysters, breaded and fried; and sweetbreads, larded, glacé.

The fruits of victory, so gloriously won on the ball field, were sweet, indeed.

But the winning ways of the Red Stockings, remarkably, did not end with the season of 1869. In 1870, the team stretched its chain of victories still farther; that is, until the fateful day of June 14, when the Cincinnati nine suffered its first defeat in two seasons at the hands of the crack Atlantic Base Ball Club of Brooklyn, New York.

Harper's Weekly, in its issue of July 2, 1870, recorded the historic loss as follows:

The New York admirers of this most manly and healthful of all athletic outdoor games were treated last week to the finest sport ever witnessed in this vicinity, in the series of matches played between the "Red Stockings," of Cincinnati, and several of our own most celebrated clubs. The "Red Stockings" came here with a reputation of little less than invincibility. They had not been defeated in two years. Their organization was splendid, their training excellent, and their confidence well grounded on a long series of triumphs over worthy competitors.

The first game took place on the Union grounds with the "Mutuals," a club with which the "Red Stockings" played a very close game last year. Then the score stood: "Red Stockings," 4; "Mutuals," 2; but this year the former had the game all their own way, and easily defeated their opponents, the score standing at the close as follows:

	1	2	3	4	5	6	7	8	9		
Red Stockings ..	0	0	2	3	3	2	4	2	0	—	16
Mutuals	0	0	0	0	0	1	1	1	0	—	3

The second game was played the following day with the "Atlantics," on the Capitoline grounds, on Long Island. From twelve to fifteen thousand people passed into the inclosure to witness the sport; and we are sorry to say that the crowd was boisterous and noisy, and greatly marred the pleasure of the game for those who wished to look on quietly. The "Red Stockings" were not treated with the courtesy they had hitherto received, and for the first, and, we trust, the last time, partisan feeling was allowed to display itself on the Capitoline

THE MATCH BETWEEN THE "RED STOCKINGS" AND THE "ATLANTICS."
From *Harper's Weekly*, July 2, 1870.

grounds, and to interfere with fair play. The "Red Stockings" conducted themselves like gentlemen, and played from first to last with
pluck and spirit. But the Fates and the crowd were against them;
and, after one of the most exciting contests on record, the victory
which seemed to be within their grasp was wrested from them, and
they retired from the field defeated, but without dishonor. The
"Atlantics" played with great skill and precision, and there is no
reason to suppose that they lent any countenance to the partisan
proceedings of the spectators. The following is the score of this
remarkable game:

	1	2	3	4	5	6	7	8	9	10	11		
Red Stockings	2	0	1	0	0	0	2	0	0	0	2	—	7
Atlantics	0	0	0	2	0	2	0	1	0	0	3	—	8

Years later, Timothy Hayes Murnane, once a baseball player himself,
and then a sports writer, shed additional light on the final play of the
game. This is of especial interest because, according to Murnane, that play
"would have shut off the winning run for the Atlantics but for a muff by
Allison at the home plate," and the Red Stocking winning streak would
not have been terminated then and there. Murnane wrote:

The ninth inning resulted in five runs each [a tie]; the tenth was
a blank; Cincinnati made two runs in the eleventh, and felt sure
of the game. With two men on bases, "old reliable" Joe Start hit the
ball in among the spectators at right field, they having crowded in
on the field. The people were in sympathy with the Brooklyn men,

and McVey had a hard time getting the ball. He pushed his way clear after a great struggle, just as Start had turned third base and was headed for home, with the crowd cheering him on.

With a short step and a swing, McVey's arm shot out like a piston rod, and the ball went as straight as a bullet into the catcher's hands, where it was dropped, just as Start rolled over the plate with the winning run, exhausted and out of breath. With one great roar and rush, the immense crowd was on the field in an instant, and Joe was hoisted upon the shoulders of several, and carried in this manner to the club-house. The joy of the crowd was in great contrast with the dismay of the Cincinnati boys, who had met with their first defeat in two seasons . . .

JOE START
Enterprise of Brooklyn, 1860
Atlantics 1861-1871

GEORGE WRIGHT
1878

With all due respect to Murnane and his exciting account of this last play, the truth of the matter is that this was not precisely the way it happened. Indeed, it was not Joe Start who scored the winning run in such a breathless manner, but Ferguson, the Atlantics' catcher, who scored on an ordinary error by Sweasy, the Cincinnati second baseman, who muffed a throw by George Wright trying for a double play on Hall's grounder to short.

The authority for this latter version is the actual description of the eleventh-inning action taken from the June 14 news dispatch to the Cincinnati *Commercial*, which reads as follows:

ATLANTICS—The chances of the Atlantics tieing seemed very slender, but they did tie and win by sheer hard hitting. Smith to first on a grounder to left field. Start struck a ball to right field into the crowd, far over McVey's head, and made third on it. In pushing the crowd aside to get the ball, McVey was kicked at by a scoundrel who had previously tried to kick the ball further off. (The scoundrel was clubbed by a policeman for this act.) Chapman out at first by Waterman. Ferguson to first by a hit past second, that, not being stopped, won the game. Start home. Zettlein to first on a fine hit to right field. Ferguson to second. Hall to first on a grounder, stopped by George Wright, who fielded it to Sweasy to put out Zettlein and Hall. Sweasy let the ball drop, and Ferguson shot over the home plate. The crowd rose and vented its joy in shouts, gratulating furiously, and throwing up hats. Pike's fly was caught by Sweasy, who sent it to George Wright, at second, before Zettlein could return— double play and side out. Three runs.

The curious fact, however, is that despite the conflicting accounts of this momentous last inning, the fabulous Cincinnati winning streak might still not have ended on that particular day—as Tim Murnane meant to emphasize in his narrative—but for a reason entirely different from the one Murnane advanced.

What might have happened is that the game could have been declared a tie, with neither side actually winning or losing, for at the end of the nine innings, the score stood deadlocked at five runs apiece. Under the then-existing rules, such a conclusion was possible, provided the captain of each team consented to a draw.

In this case, however, Harry Wright, the Cincinnati captain, refused to agree. He insisted that the game continue until one side or another achieved a victory on the ballfield, or that Cincinnati be declared the winner by default—this, despite the fact that the Atlantic club directors, captain, and players were all eager and willing to have the game declared a draw. To have been able to stand off the redoubtable Red Stockings to an undisputed tie would have been victory enough for them. Indeed, while the lengthy discussion between the team captains was going on, almost all of the Atlantic players had left the field, gone to their lockers, and changed their uniforms.

GEORGE WRIGHT
1868

HARRY WRIGHT
1868

Red Stocking adorning menu of
celebration dinner accorded to
the celebrated team of Cincinnati, 1869.

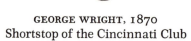

GEORGE WRIGHT, 1870
Shortstop of the Cincinnati Club

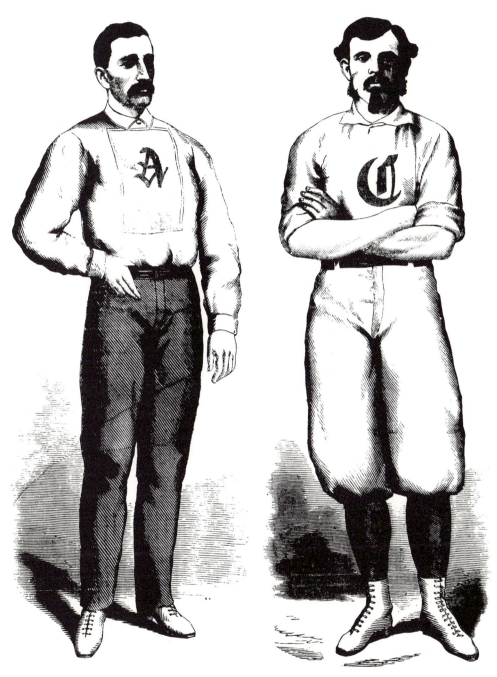

ROBERT FERGUSON, 1870
Captain and Catcher of Atlantic Club

HARRY WRIGHT, 1870
Captain and Centre Field of Cincinnati Club

Official boxscore of the game that broke the Red Stockings
two-year winning streak, June 14, 1870

When it became evident that no agreement could be reached to terminate the game in an amicable tie, the Atlantic players were recalled to the field, and the game was resumed. Thus, because the Red Stockings were so determined to secure yet another victory, the longest winning streak in baseball history was abruptly ended. Harry Wright had simply pushed his team's luck too far.

Meanwhile, the celebrated exploits of the Red Stockings were not merely recorded as so many baseball statistics. On the contrary, they had

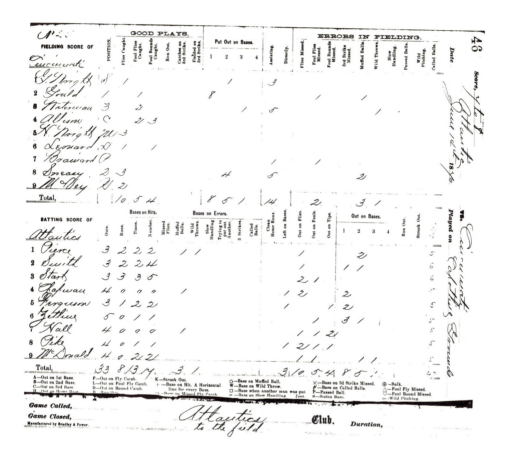

a deep and direct influence on the game in general. The impact was almost immediate and far-reaching in character. For, since they were the first openly admitted, fully professional baseball club, the Red Stockings, by their gentlemanly behavior and skillful play, lent a degree of respectability to professional ball-playing that formerly had been lacking in the sport.

This, in turn, gave impetus to the formation of other fully professional teams; by the start of the 1870 season, a number of prominent clubs had openly declared themselves as patrons of the professional system. Among these were the following: Atlantic of Brooklyn; Athletic of Philadelphia; White Stockings of Chicago; Eckford of Brooklyn; Keystone of Philadelphia; Mutual of New York; National of Washington; Olympic of Baltimore; Tri-Mountain of Boston; Union of Lansingburg; and Union of Morrisania.

In addition, a host of other baseball organizations throughout the nation continued to play the game on a semiprofessional basis. The wholly amateur clubs had more or less faded from the public sporting scene; and with them, there slowly passed into history the parent amateur body—the National Association of Base Ball Players.

With the rise of professional baseball and the approach of the decade of the seventies, the time now appeared ripe for new developments in the national pastime. And on the changing baseball horizon, these were already taking shape.

A form of gymnasium exercise for baseball players in the 1880s

EIGHT

◆

BIRTH

OF THE

NATIONAL LEAGUE

Early in 1870, the Bombay *Gazette* announced that the government of India had received word from Dr. David Livingstone, the African explorer, that he believed he had discovered the unknown sources of the River Nile at approximately the position assigned to them by Ptolemy, the ancient Greek geographer.

In the political and military circles of Europe, the stage was rapidly being readied for the outbreak and pursuit of the Franco-Prussian War.

And in the United States, hectic preparations were being carried forth throughout the land for the approaching baseball season.

Reviewing developments regarding the national pastime, *The New York Times,* in an April editorial, said:

> During the past Winter professional circles have been greatly excited at times in consequence of the strenuous exertions made by rival professional clubs to secure the strongest nines, the means adopted to add players to their lists not always being of a creditable character. Of course, all professionals have a right to better their positions at the close of each season, by changing from one club to another; and several first-class players have done so this past Winter, and without

loss of reputation. But the class known as "revolvers" change from one club to another, getting all they can out of each, and breaking regular engagements and written contracts without hesitation and with impunity. We are glad to learn, however, that the leading clubs have determined to adopt a rule this Spring which will be a severe blow to this revolving business, and the rule in question is . . . not to play a single match with any club in whose nine there is a player who has broken his written engagement to any club, or who, in other words, is a "revolver."

In effect, what the *Times* was saying was that abuses of various sorts had begun to creep into the sport. Since professionalism was now an openly recognized fact, there no longer was any real necessity for either players or clubs to conduct secret negotiations regarding their playing commitments. So far as the players were concerned, because they were playing the game for a livelihood, they were prepared to sign with any club offering the most money, even if it meant "revolving" from club to club in order to obtain it.

Regarding the clubs' responsibility in the matter, because of their eagerness to come up with winning ball teams, they were prepared to extend more and more alluring offers to the players in order to secure the ones they wanted.

The net result was that the clubs found themselves in the paradoxical position of perpetuating and fostering the very evil they now were being confronted with—namely, a growing lack of stability in the sport.

Complicating matters, the general public, for their part, was becoming increasingly demanding and hard to please. People wanted more and more excitement in their daily lives; and this, in turn, was being reflected in their attitude toward sports.

Taking note of this growing tendency, *The Western Monthly*, a Chicago publication, in its issue of November 1870, asked:

Why is it that the American people must always rush to extremes in everything—that they can never hit the happy medium in anything to which they apply themselves? A few years ago we neglected physical exercise; and now, having discovered our mistake, we fly to the opposite extreme . . . Walking, we seem to think is nothing, unless we climb the dizzy heights of Washington or Mansfield, or travel a hundred miles in a hundred hours; boating amounts to nothing, unless we nearly burst a blood vessel; and *base-ball* is nothing, unless we go mad with excitement on the subject, and the whole land is covered with clubs that affiliate, and compete, and work with all the zeal of political champions.

Then, answering its own rhetorical question, the periodical continued:

All this strikes us as very foolish. We live in an age of snobbery and brag, and there is a general tendency to despise any pursuit which has not cost a mint of money, or consumed a large amount of energy, or which does not somehow stand out in a signal and boastful manner. Because physical vigor is a good thing, it does not follow that one must have the digestion of an ostrich, the strength of an ox, or the lungs of a race-horse . . . There is a limit beyond which too much is as bad as too little exercise. The kind of training to which many Americans subject themselves may give them temporarily superior physical power over their fellows, but it will be at the expense of their brains . . . it is a superiority for which they will pay in middle age with stiffened sinews and rheumatic joints, compelling them to hobble about like broken-down canal-horses.

So much for the "participating" segment of the public. However, the developing "athletic craze," as it now was beginning to be called, was rapidly infecting the remaining portion of the population—the spectators. If people did not actively participate, they at least watched others exert themselves. And if it was often necesary to pay a certain fee for the privilege of being a spectator, that in itself did not deter many individuals.

In connection with the national pastime, the "craze" was termed "base ball fever." Superficially, this would appear to have been a relatively mild affliction. However, in the manner it was developing—especially in professional competition—the fever gave rise to other more serious ailments—pool-playing, gambling, chicanery, and fraud.

In the same issue cited above, *The Western Monthly* discussed aspects of the problem in the following colorful style:

To appreciate the importance of Base Ball as a Business, one has but to visit Dexter Park in Chicago, or the Capitoline grounds at Brooklyn, on the occasion of an important match game. Say it is Dexter Park. Two or three extra trains are run on each of the two railroads leading from the city to the Park. Each train is packed like a train of cattle-cars. Besides this, the street cars and every acessible buggy and barouche in town are brought into requisition, and the thoroughfares leading to the Park are the scene of a continuous caravan of vehicles and dust. The receipts at the gate often reach several thousand dollars. Those at the match between the Chicagos and the Forest Cities at Dexter Park in June exceeded five thousand dollars; and those at the match between the Chicagos and Atlantics, at New York on the Fourth of July, were still larger—the Chicago party taking fourteen hundred and fifty dollars as their quarter share.

The immense audience disposed, for the most part, on the seats of the "grand stand," a favored hundred or two in the cool piazzas and balconies of the Club House; an adverturous Gideon's band, mostly made up of sports, amateur and professional, congregating in front of the Club House, a score of reporters thrown out, like a company of skirmishers, well into the field, and the remainder of the throng scattered promiscuously about the skirts of the field, in carriages or otherwise,—the game commences. If it happens to run pretty evenly, or even if the score is kept down to a low figure, the interest of the crowd is intense. Every good play of any member on either side is hailed with huzzas, partly from amateurs who admire the feat, but chiefly from betters who have put money on the players' side. At the end of each inning the ears of those in the vicinity of the Club House are saluted with all sorts of propositions for wagers. A stolid-looking fellow with a big neck wants to "go another fifty" on the Ultramarines. A small individual with a sharp nose, a quid of tobacco, and a pocket-handkerchief tied about his neck, desires to hazard a hundred dollars that the Pea Greens don't make three more runs. A terribly excited young man, who has evidently had some training at grain-gambling but little at field sports, announces, in a voice quivering with excitement, his willingness to hazard ten to fifteen on the Pea Greens. Anon somebody makes a proposition which is received with a general hoot and a suggestion to "soak your head." The same demonstrations occur, in a less degree, in other parts of the Park. In fact, two-thirds of the persons in the vast throng have money or hats—which, unfortunately cost money,—hazarded on the game, and every heart is beating high for the deciding event. It seems as if each of those ten thousand hearts had received the pulsation and momentum of all the others. At length the game is over. Those who went purely to see the sport have enjoyed without distraction a fair exhibition of manly skill and strength, and just a healthy degree of excitement. Those who foolishly put their means at hazard have had too much anxiety for enjoyment, and come away glowing or gloomy, according to their luck.

The picture painted by the *Monthly* was by no means an exaggeration of prevailing conditions; nor was it an isolated situation confined to baseball competition in Chicago. If anything, conditions were a good deal worse and, unfortunately, widespread.

At the close of the 1870 season, *The New York Times* sounded a brief editorial note of concern: "Certain evils," said the *Times*, "have followed in the train of professional ball playing, which, if not checked in their progress, will ultimately so damage the reputation of the fraternity as to materially interfere with the future welfare of the game."

Several months later, in January of 1871, the newspaper further implemented its warning. "The number of stock base-ball companies now incorporated," observed the *Times*, "shows that over $100,000 has been invested in this business for the coming year. Under these circumstances it becomes necessary for club managers to take a strong stand in opposition to the hippodroming business which was indulged in to a considerable extent last season."

About the very same time, a dispatch from Europe, where the Franco-Prussian conflict was raging, showed that even in the "game" of war, certain ungentlemanly practices were creeping into play. The dispatch read: "London. Jan. 14.—The French Foreign Office has protested against the bombardment of Paris, on the ground that it was commenced without the formal notification required by the usages of civilized warfare."

The age, apparently, was suffering from a growing deterioration of moral values and principles that covered the broad spectrum of human relationships, ranging all the way from contests on the battlefield to contests on the playing field.

Finally, shortly before the start of the new baseball season, *The New York Times,* in a March report, spelled out what it previously had referred to as "certain evils" and "the hippodroming business;" this is what it said:

> A sad change has taken place in the status of the game, and in the place of enjoyable amateur contests, witnessed by crowds of ladies, and governed only by the incentives of an honorable effort to win the simple trophy of the game, we have seen a field crowded with thousands of people who have paid an admission fee to the grounds, and the game patronized by the worst classes of the community, of both sexes; and, moreover, many of the gatherings have been characterized by the presence of a regular gambling horde, while oaths and obscenity have prevailed, and fraudulent combinations of one kind or another have marked the arrangements connected with some of the prominent contests. Of course there have been many exceptions to this rule, but the fact is patent to every lover of the game that the effect of this amalgamation of all classes of the fraternity into one, including all the existing evil associations, has been to drive

HEADQUARTERS
OF THE
Kekionga Base Ball Club,

Fort Wayne, Ind., April 15th, 1871.

Mr. *Harry Wright*

Sec'y *Nat'l Association*

    We take pleasure in announcing to you that our Professional Club is now in condition to meet all first class clubs, and herewith invite your club to visit us, guaranteeing that all will prove most satisfactory. Our Grounds have been greatly improved this season, and can assure you they are second to none in America. Fort Wayne is the terminus of seven Rail Roads, and numbers over twenty-five thousand inhabitants. Therefore, should you favor us with a visit, we advise that as early notice as possible be sent us so games can be properly advertised. Will grant in all games one-half net receipts, and expect the same in return. Make our Western Tour in June; Eastern Tour August; Southern Tour October.

KEKIONGA NINE.

ROBERT MATTHEWS, *Pitcher.*　　FRANK WILLIAMS, *Third Base.*
WM. LENNON, *Catcher.*　　ED. MINCHER, *Left Field.*
E. H. BONKER, *Short Stop.*　　JAS. FORAN, *Centre Field.*
THOS. FORKER, *First Base.*　　THOMAS CAREY, *Right Field.*
W. GOLDSMITH, *Second Base.*　　WM. KELLY, *Pitcher and Centre Field.*

    C. M. DAWSON,
    MAX NIRDLINGER,
    G. J. E. MAYERS,
    L. M. FLEMING,　　　　　　**GEO. J. E. MAYERS,**
    S. C. LUMBARD,　　　　　　*Cor. and Rec. Secretary.*
    JNO. R. HOAGLAND,
        Directors.

Kekionga Base Ball Club letter

out of the game nearly every player who used to engage in base-ball solely for pleasurable and exciting exercise. Hence we have seen club after club once prominent among the most reputable of the base-ball organizations, either become defunct altogether, or so dormant as to cease to exist as an active club.

Whether goaded by editorial rebukes such as these, or by the urgings of sports writers Henry Chadwick, in the *New York Clipper,* and Al Wright, in the *Philadelphia Mercury,* a meeting was held at last by the representatives of the major professional baseball clubs to find ways and means of again stabilizing the sport. The meeting was held on March 17, 1871, at Collier's Rooms, located at 840 Broadway, New York City, and the following ten organizations were represented: Mutuals of New York, Eckfords of Brooklyn, Athletics of Philadelphia, White Stockings of Chicago, Bostons of Boston, Haymakers of Troy, Kekiongas of Fort Wayne, Olympics of Washington, Forest City of Cleveland, and Forest City of Rockford, Illinois.

Out of this conference of professional baseball men, there emerged the first professional organization of its kind—the National Association of Professional Base Ball Players. The constitution and rules of the late amateur body were adopted, and a group of officers were elected as follows: James N. Kern, of the Athletics, president; J. S. Evans, of Forest City, Cleveland, vice-president; N. E. Young, of Olympic, Washington, secretary; and J. W. Schofield, of Haymaker, Troy, treasurer.

The new organization was practically an exact counterpart of the old National Association, and the season opened on a note of high expectations. This was slightly marred, however, when the Eckfords of Brooklyn decided not to affiliate immediately with the new national body.*

The first professional championship was won by the Athletics of Philadelphia, who finished ahead of Boston and Chicago, in that order. The Chicago players were somewhat handicapped in the latter part of the pennant race by the great calamity of 1871, for the disastrous great fire, which swept through and destroyed most of the city in October, also burned up the Chicago ball park. This forced the White Stockings to play out their final games on the road instead of in the more familiar surroundings of their home grounds. The result was that they lost their last three games in a row and wound up the season in third place.

During the first year of its existence, the new professional association managed to restore a good deal of the waning public confidence in the

* Eckford eventually joined up in midseason, replacing Kekionga, which dropped out.

DICK MCBRIDE, 1870
Captain and Pitcher of the Philadelphia Athletic Club

CHARLES PABOR, 1870
Pitcher of the Union Club, of Morrisania, N.Y.

AL REACH, 1870
Second Base of the Philadelphia Athletic Club

ATHLETICS AND PHILADELPHIA CLUBS AT PHILADELPHIA.
From *New York Daily Graphic*, April 30, 1873.

sport. Unfortunately, however, the respite from deterioration was only too brief. Before long, the old forces of evil and corruption were back at work, again undermining professional baseball. And by 1873, *The New York Times* was saying:

> We do object to calling this purely business transaction a national pastime, or a pastime at all. The young men who do the playing and fearlessly expose their manly beauty to the malignant ball, work hard enough, and probably earn their money, but it is work, and not in any real sense sport. Nor . . . do we perceive how the persons who contribute to their expenses and bet on their skill, divide their winnings, and "jockey" their matches, can be called "sportsmen," or in what way they forward the physical development of the nation. Out-door sports we have always and most earnestly advocated, and pressed upon the attention of our young men. But they ought to practice for recreation and exercise, not for gain; the rivalry they excite should be a generous and manly desire for phys-

BASEBALL IN ENGLAND. RED STOCKINGS AND ATHLETICS.
From *Harper's Weekly*, September 5, 1874.

ical superiority, not an ignoble strife for dollars. A pastime, however excellent in itself, loses all its advantages once it is degraded into a mere instrument for gambling.

In 1874, the Red Stockings of Boston and the Athletics of Philadelphia sailed to England; there, on the last two days of July and throughout the month of August, the two teams played a series of exhibition baseball games, as well as a number of cricket matches, before British audiences. This was the first major exposure of American baseball to Englishmen, and although the tour was widely reported both in the British and the American press, the affair was somewhat less than successful.

According to one description in the *St. Louis Democrat:*

A large majority of the spectators seemed immensely pleased with the game, and expressed their pleasure in good, hearty English applause. There were those, however . . . who could not be made to see anything in base ball, and who were not careful to hide their contempt for it . . . these persons were for the most part active cricketers.

THE CHAMPIONSHIP BOSTON NINE, THAT MADE THE MEMORABLE TOUR TO
EUROPE IN 1874.

PLAYING ON THE OLD TRAFFORD GROUNDS IN MANCHESTER.   COMPLIMENTARY DINNER IN LONDON GIVEN BY THE MARYLEBONE CRICKET CLUB.

THE AMERICAN BASE BALL CLUBS IN ENGLAND.
From the *London Graphic*, August 20, 1874.

One Englishwoman, who obviously was not an "active cricketer," judging from the way she signed her letter, wrote to the *London Times* on August 11 to express her feelings about the American ballplayers. This is what she said:

> *To the Editor of the Times:*
>   Sir—Some American athletes are trying to introduce to us their game of base ball, as if it were a novelty; whereas the fact is that it is an ancient English game, long ago discarded in favor of cricket.
>   In a letter of the celebrated Mary Lepel, Lady Harvey, written in 1748, the family of Frederick, Prince of Wales, are described as "diverting themselves with base-ball, a play all who are or have been schoolboys are well acquainted with."
>
> Your obedient servant,
Grandmother.

Here, once again, was another claim that baseball was known long before Abner Doubleday was supposed to have invented the game—indeed, at least 91 years before.

So much for the overseas tour of 1874. However, this, plus the fact that the Boston team won its third straight Association pennant, were the two baseball highlights of the year.

In 1875, by again winning the championship, the Bostons made it four triumphs in a row. Indeed, simply beating Boston had become an end in itself, evoking all the local pride, passion, and excitement that had prevailed during 1869 and 1870, when the invincible Cincinnati Red Stockings made an appearance in town.

A Sure Way for the Bostons to Beat the Chicagos is to Shoot them Out

In 1876 Chicago left Boston in the lurch, capturing the first National League championship, with 52 games won and only 14 lost

It is not surprising, therefore, that when the Bostons were shut out one afternoon by Chicago, 2–0, that the Windy City fans went wild. This is how the *Chicago Times,* on June 9th, ecstatically headlined its report:

TEAR DOWN BUNKER HILL.

For the Glory of Its Base-Ball
Representatives Has
Departed.

And Their Proud Championship
Banner is Plastered with
Whitewash.

A Liberal Coat of Which Was
Administered Yesterday by
the Erratic Chicagos.

But of even greater significance than all this, the year 1875 also saw the groundwork laid for a new professional circuit—the National League of Professional Base Ball Clubs, popularly known as the National League.

It is of more than routine interest to note that, oddly, this new organization, which subsequently became a potent force for baseball reform, was itself originally a product of some intricate behind-the-scenes conniving in the grand manner.

In 1875, William A. Hulbert became president of the Chicago White Stockings. Being an ardent baseball fan, as well as a dynamic businessman

WILLIAM A. HULBERT
Organizer of the National League

of the West, Hulbert determined to wrest the baseball championship from the New England city of Boston and bring it inland to Chicago. This he proceeded to do in the most direct manner he believed possible, which was to attempt to acquire for Chicago the most talented athletes in the game— namely, the very same ballplayers who were repeatedly winning the championship for Boston.

To state it another way, what Hulbert had in mind was a "talent raid" on the Boston club, by means of which he would bring to Chicago the outstanding baseball stars of Boston. This he succeeded in doing by secretly signing up Boston's "Big Four" players—A. G. Spalding, the best Association pitcher; Ross Barnes, star second baseman; and Calvin McVey and "Deacon" Jim White, veteran catchers.

When news of Hulbert's coup leaked out, a great furor was raised in the Massachusetts capital. Rumors flew to the effect that Chicago, for its "unethical action," would be expelled from the National Association. However, considering the much more serious abuses that were tolerated, Hulbert had little to fear in that respect. Nevertheless, to insure himself against that eventuality, he came up with the plan of forming an altogether

ALBERT G. SPALDING
Pitcher for Boston, 1871; pitcher and manager for Chicago, 1876-7.
Together with Hulbert, he helped organize the National League.
From an old portrait—*Root & Tinker, Tribune Building, N.Y. 1884.*

new circuit of clubs in which his team of athletes would be able to play and compete for a baseball championship.

Because of the evils that were infesting the sport, the idea of "reform" held an especially strong psychological appeal. Keenly aware of this, Hulbert invited the presidents of all National Association clubs to a meeting to consider measures of mutual interest in connection with rehabilitating the national pastime.

The meeting was held in New York City on February 2, 1876; and Hulbert, acting as spokesman for the four Western clubs—Chicago, Louisville, Cincinnati, and St. Louis—met with the leaders of the four Eastern outfits—New York, Philadelphia, Hartford, and Boston. After describing the evil state of affairs rampant in the sport and then presenting a program for reform, the astute Chicago magnate offered for consideration a new baseball constitution plus a standard player's contract, both of which had previously been drawn up by Judge Orrick C. Bishop of St. Louis.

Although from the start of the conference he was faced by an antagonistic group of Eastern executives, by the time the meeting ended, the Westerner's persuasiveness, apparent sincerity, and concrete proposals finally carried the day. And out of that historic conference in New York, the National League of Professional Base Ball Clubs was born.

Morgan G. Bulkeley, of Hartford, was elected to the League's first presidency, and the old National Association was permitted to expire of its own accord.

Thus, one hundred years after the start of the American Revolution— which conflict marked the founding of the nation—a revolutionary new beginning took place in the structure of the American national pastime. And a new era of baseball was thereby ushered in.

I being in very poor circumstances at the present writing, out of employment, and am unable to pay my expenses as I am about 3 weeks behind on my board. hoping you will oblige me by sending me $15.00 and I will promise you

NINE

PROFESSIONAL CRISES
AND
CONFLICTS

It must not be thought that simply because a new league of professional baseball clubs was organized in 1876 that the national pastime suddenly and automatically was also raised above the quagmire of corruption and decay in which it had been wallowing for years. For notwithstanding the fact that the constitution of the new National League stated, "The object of this organization is to encourage, foster, and elevate the game of baseball . . . and to make baseball playing respectable and honorable," the projected task of reform was both difficult and formidable of accomplishment.

As if to substantiate this, on September 21, 1876, *The New York Times,* under the heading, "A Disgraceful Scene on the Union Grounds," printed the following baseball dispatch:

> Early in the afternoon the betting in the pool-room was 25 to 10 in favor of the New-York team, but just before the game began these odds turned in favor of the Brooklyn men. At this time it was openly asserted that at least two of the New-York players had arranged to lose the game, and the subsequent exhibition of fielding on the part of the two mentioned certainly gave color to the charge . . . Rule

and Fallon, the two pitchers, [finally] shook hands, and refusing longer to engage in such a disgraceful affair walked off of the field. At the solicitation of the two Captains the umpire called the affair a draw. While the players were changing their uniforms in the club-house some one accused Hovey of selling the game. A disgraceful fight ensued, to suppress which the Police had to be called in, a fitting finale to the most disreputable proceeding that has been witnessed on a ball field in this vicinity for years.

In short, despite the League's professed intent to "elevate the game," pool-playing, gambling, dishonesty, and disorderliness still were haunting the pastime. And to further complicate matters, even though the League had prohibited the sale of intoxicating beverages on club grounds (one of the various prior-existing evils), many ballplayers were not averse to buy-ing and drinking beer and liquor elsewhere—a personal habit which naturally and frequently affected their playing ability on the diamond.

By 1870, the cover had been adorned with players.

In an effort to cope with this particular aspect of the many-sided baseball problem, *Beadle's Dime Centennial Base-Ball Player*, a popular guidebook of the period, printed these practical lines of advice:

Any man now desirous of using his physical and mental powers to their utmost advantage, must ignore first, intemperance in eating, and second, refuse to allow a drop of alcoholic liquor, whether in the form of spirits, wine or beer, to pass down his throat. We are not preaching "temperance" to the fraternity, but telling them facts, hard, incontrovertible facts, which experience is gradually proving to those who have charge of the training of athletes . . . How many ball-players . . . at match after match, are deluded into the notion that by drinking whiskey in the midst of their game, they thereby impart new vigor to their bodies, clear their judgment and sight, and inspirit them to greater endurance, when the undeniable fact is, that the liquor they drink does the very reverse of all these things, as it neither nourishes the system nor clears the sight; on the contrary, inflames the stomach, clouds the brain, and actually weakens the whole man.

LOUIS SOCKALEXIS (Louis Frances) "Chief"
1897-9 Cleveland Nationals, outfield. 3-year average .313

Still, it was one thing to print or to give advice, and another to have that advice heeded. Unfortunately, for season after season, drunkenness among the players continued to be a major source of anxiety to team managers, captains, and club owners alike.

Even after the turn of the century, in the days when the great Christy Mathewson was hurling his way into diamond history, hard drinking was still being decried in various ways, as, for example, in W. F. Kirk's mournful temperance ballad, "John Bourbon, Pitcher":

> They tell me that Matty can pitch like a fiend,
> But many long years before Matty was weaned
> I was pitching to players, and good players, too,
> Mike Kelley and Rusie and all the old crew.
> Red Sockalexis, the Indian star,
> Breitenstein, Clancey, McGill and McGarr.
> Matty a pitcher? Well, yes, he may be,
> But where in the world is a pitcher like me?

> My name is John Bourbon, I'm old, and yet young;
> I cannot keep track of the victims I've stung.
> I've studied their weaknesses, humored their whims,
> Muddled their eyesight and weakened their limbs,
> Bloated their faces and dammed up their veins,
> Rusted their joints and beclouded their brains.
> Matty a pitcher? Well, yes, he may be,
> But where in the world is a pitcher like me?

> I have pitched to the stars of our national game,
> I have pitched them to ruin and pitched them to shame.
> They laughed when they faced me, so proud of their strength,
> Not knowing, poor fools, I would get them at length.
> I have pitched men off pinnacles scaled in long years.
> I have pitched those they loved into oceans of tears.
> Matty a pitcher? Well, yes, he may be,
> But where in the world is a pitcher like me?

The first real break in the campaign to restore general confidence in professional baseball materialized during the year 1877, when William A. Hulbert, the new League president, banned from the sport for life four players of the Louisville Club who were found guilty of conspiring with gamblers to deliberately lose games for a fee.

The players involved in the scandal were James A. Devlin, William H. Craver, George Hall, and Albert H. Nichols.

Hall had played the outfield for the Atlantics on that memorable day in 1870 when the New York team stopped the Cincinnati Red Stockings' two-season winning streak. He also had been a member of the Boston team when, together with the Athletics of Philadelphia, they made the first American baseball tour to England in 1874.

Craver was a veteran catcher, one of the breed who doggedly stood up close to the bat in the days before the catcher's mask or glove came into use. He was once described as "the patentee of the foul tip," and his face, it was said, looked like that of a badly battered boxer.

GEORGE HALL.
Boston outfielder in 1874. Banned for life from professional baseball, together with Devlin, Craver, and Nichols, for conspiring with gamblers to lose games for a fee.

Nichols was an all-around infielder, having played every position in the infield—first, second, third, and short—for the Atlantics, Mutuals, and Louisville.

But it was Devlin who probably lost the most from the scandal, for he had been on his way to one of the finest reputations in baseball. A fast-ball pitcher, in 1876 he had won 30 games for Louisville, and in 1877, 35.

It was also Devlin who, of the four players, was the hardest hit financially. Uneducated and relatively illiterate, the best thing he was able to do was to play baseball, and the opportunity to do this was now being denied to him for life.

Among the correspondence of Harry Wright, the manager and secretary of the old Boston Base Ball Club, there still exists the original letter that Devlin sent him from Philadelphia, on February 24, 1878, pleading for understanding and help. The letter is probably one of the most pathetic and poignant documents of its type ever written. With all of its mistakes in English, spelling, and punctuation, this is exactly the way it reads:

> *Phila   Feb 24th 1878*
> *Mr Harry Wright*
> *   Dear Sir*
>
> *as I am Deprived from Playing this year I thought I woed [would]*
> *write you to see if you Coed [could] do anything for me in the*
> *way of looking after your ground or anything in the way of work*
> *I Dont Know what I am to do   I have tried hard to get work of*
> *any Kind   But I Canot get it   do you Know of anyway that you*
> *think I Coed [could] get to Play again   I Can asure you Harry*
> *that I was not Treated right and if Ever I Can see you to tell*
> *you the Case you will say I am not to Blame   I am living from*
> *hand to mouth all winter   I have not got a Stich of Clothing*
> *or has my wife and child   You Dont Know how I am Situated for*
> *I Know if you did you woed [would] do Something for me   I am*
> *honest Harry   you need not Be afraid   the Louisville People made*
> *me what I am to day   a Begger   I trust you will not Say anything*
> *to anyone about the Contents of this to any one   if you Can do*
> *me this favor By letting me take Care of the ground or anything*
> *of that Kind   I Beg of you to do it   and god will reward you*
> *if I Dont   or let me Know if you have any Ide [idea] of how I*
> *Coed [could] get Back   I am Dumb Harry   I dont Know how to go*
> *about it   So I Trust you will answear this and do all you Can*
> *for me   So I will Close by Sending you & Geo and all the Boys*
> *my verry Best wishes   hoping to hear from you Soon   I am yours*
> *Trouly*
>
> *   James A Devlin*
> *   No 908   Atherton St*
> *   Phila   Pa*

Years later, Albert G. Spalding described a scene he had witnessed by chance from a room adjoining the office of William A. Hulbert, the president of the League; James Devlin had come to plead his cause in person, and he had fallen on his knees:

His lips gave utterance to such a plea for mercy as might have come from one condemned to the gallows . . . It was a scene of heart-rending tragedy. Devlin was in tears, Hulbert was in tears . . . I heard Devlin's plea to have the stigma removed from his name. I heard him entreat, not on his own account—he acknowledged himself unworthy of consideration—but for the sake of his wife and child . . . I saw the President's hand steal into his pocket as if seeking to conceal his intended act from the other hand. I saw him take a $50 bill and press it into the palm of the prostrate player. And then I heard him say, as he fairly writhed with the pain his own words caused him, "That's what I think of you, personally; but, damn you, Devlin, you are dishonest; you have sold a game, and I can't trust you. Now go; and let me never see your face again; for your act will not be condoned so long as I live."

The ousted players repeatedly tried to have themselves reinstated, but to no avail. At a League meeting, held on December 8, 1880, after a motion concerning removal of the disabilities of Nichols, Hall, Craver, and Devlin, the following resolution was read and adopted:

RESOLVED, That notice is hereby served on the persons named, and on their friends, defenders and apologists, that the Board of Directors of the National League will *never* remit the penalties inflicted on such persons, nor will they hereafter entertain any appeal from them or in their behalf.

Actually, the case of the "Louisville quartette," as the men came to be known, was not the first instance of players being banned from baseball for crookedness, nor was it the last.

The first case on record concerned a game played on September 28, 1865 (barely six months after the close of the Civil War) between the old Eckford and Mutual baseball clubs. The players involved were Thomas H. Devyr, E. Duffy, and William Wansley, all members of the Mutuals. The three players had conspired with two men, Kane McLaughlin and S. O'Donnell, to deliberately and fraudulently lose the second game of a three-game series between the two clubs. The facts of the conspiracy were set forth in an affidavit that was signed on November 1, 1865, before George H. McKay, a notary public. Later that month, the three men, convicted of the conspiracy, were formally expelled from their club.

In this first case of baseball conspiracy, however, the banishment of the players did not prove to be permanent. Since neither the Eckford Club nor the Mutual Club was anxious to publicize the scandal, neither ever brought a formal complaint before the judiciary committee of the National Association, the then-governing body of baseball. Consequently, in one way or another, the players continued to participate in the sport. And, in the case of Tom Devyr at least, there was even a curious sequel, for he not only managed to have himself readmitted to membership in the Mutuals, but, in 1867, when the legitimacy of his membership was challenged, he succeeded in having the charges against him dismissed with a declaration that no convincing evidence had been presented at the hearing to show that he had ever conspired to sell a game.

Oddly, the Mutual Club in 1867 strongly supported Devyr's position, although in 1865 that very club had expelled him for fraud. The reason, perhaps, lies in the fact that by having readmitted an expelled player to membership, under the rules, the club itself had become liable to expulsion from the National Association. In defending Devyr, therefore, the Mutuals actually were defending themselves.

In retrospect, it is not too surprising that the Mutual Club was connected with such unsavory proceedings, nor that it could extricate itself so adroitly from embarrassing situations, for the organization was one of the most influential and powerful clubs of its time, and deeply involved in the dirty politics of New York. Mutual patrons included members of Tammany Hall, city judges, city councilmen, and various other officials of the corrupt "Boss" Tweed regime.

It was in 1869, in fact, that Boss Tweed's aldermen even voted a $1,500 appropriation out of the city's treasury, designed to support its favorite baseball club. The preamble and resolution to the effect read as follows:

> WHEREAS, It has been the custom of the municipal authorities of several cities in the United States to encourage, by legislative action, such pastimes and pleasures among their immediate citizens as tend to their physical benefit and education; and,
>
> WHEREAS, The increase for outdoor pastimes among the young men of this city, productive as they are of a moral, intellectual and physical advantage, merits encouragement at the hands of this common council; therefore be it
>
> RESOLVED, That a joint special committee of five members from each branch of the common council be appointed to procure suitable prizes to be competed for under their supervision by such regularly organized associations of this city having for their object athletic pastimes as the

said committee may select, including, however, rowing and baseball playing, and that the sum of $1,500 be and the same is hereby appropriated to carry out the provisions of this resolution, and the same charged to the appropriation for city contingencies.

The most celebrated case of baseball corruption, of course, occurred many years after the "Louisville quartette" affair; and it shook the baseball world to its very foundations. The scandal broke in 1920, and its dimensions not only shocked the nation, but, in addition, all but sounded the death knell for the professional game. To the dismay of all true sportslovers, it was disclosed that eight members of the Chicago White Sox (subsequently called the "Black Sox") had conspired with a gambling syndicate to deliberately lose the World Series of 1919 to the Cincinnati Nationals.

The players involved in the scandal were "Shoeless" Joe Jackson, Charles "Chick" Gandil, "Happy" Oscar Felsch, Ed Cicotte, Fred McMullin, Claude Williams, George "Buck" Weaver, and Charles "Swede" Risberg. Of the lot, as it turned out, it was Ed Cicotte alone who had actually received money for his role in the conspiracy—the sum of $10,000. In the 43-year interval between the Louisville case and the Black Sox scandal, the sellout price had risen exactly one hundredfold, for James A. Devlin had received only $100 to commit the fraud that eventually ruined his life.

In the aftermath of the Black Sox scandal, as in 1877, all the players involved in the conspiracy were banned from the sport forever. In 1877, however, the situation in baseball was much more difficult and delicate. Hulbert was struggling to redeem a sport that for years had been plagued by gambling and corruption. An indication of his serious purpose was manifest long before the case of the Louisville quartette. This was evident in the example he set by lifting the playing franchises of the New York and Philadelphia clubs for not fulfilling their first season's game commitments in the West out of fear of incurring financial losses on the road. To Hulbert, the clubs' monetary problems were of secondary concern; as he viewed the matter, it was far more important that the League's reputation, as well as its authority, not be lost in the initial year of its existence.

The extent to which he succeeded in placing the League on a firm and respectable footing is embodied in the brief resolution adopted by the organization on the occasion of Hulbert's death in 1882: "*Resolved*—That to him alone is due the credit of having founded the National League, and to his able leadership, sound judgment, and impartial management is the success of the League chiefly due."

1877 circular.
Even in the last century, before radio and television,
the value of publicity and personal appearances was recognized.

It must be borne in mind, however, that when Hulbert died, the League had been in existence only a mere six years. The "success," therefore, is to be measured broadly within a relatively narrow framework of time; for during that six-year period, the League was in a more or less constant state of ferment. That this was so has already been demonstrated, but other examples are on record that merit discussion.

In 1879, for instance, sufficient public confidence had been restored by the League that the possession of a winning ball team again had become a matter of community pride. This, naturally, was expressed through sundry means, but one of the most revealing, historically, is the printed record left behind by the contemporary press of the various communities. And one of the most curious of such records—remembering the pride of Cincinnati in her champion Red Stockings of 1869—is what the Cincinnati *Commercial* had to say about the city's baseball team ten years later, in June 1879:

Roaming somewhere around in the Eastern states, like an animal without a keeper is an organization claiming to represent the base ball talent of Cincinnati, the Paris of America. Occasionally a telegram is received from some city of the third-class in regard to the team, announcing that it has had the temerity to contest with the home nine for victory and been deservedly whipped for it. Cincinnatians take it all in good part, as they are now getting accustomed to such intelligence. When the club returns from its eastern tour it will alight from the train at midnight at some point outside of the city and make its way into town in detachments by different routes over the hill-tops. It is reported that disguises have been purchased by the individual players for use on arrival.

But Cincinnati was not unique in expressions of disdain regarding its baseball nine. The city of Chicago, Cincinnati's arch rival, was equally colorful and blunt in its comments about its baseball club, which had distinguished itself by winning the League's first championship in 1876. However, this was now August 1879, and the Chicago team was in the throes of a losing streak that had gradually taken it from first to third place in the pennant race. This was what the Chicago *Tribune* said:

It is a pretty well known fact that during the past two weeks the aggregation of base ball talent variously known as the Chicagos, the White Stockings, the Silk Stockings, Anson's Gang, Hulbert's Hired Men, etc., have been bringing disgrace upon this city and execrations upon their own heads by the extraordinarily capable manner in which they have allowed themselves to be beaten by clubs which a few weeks ago they would have scorned to acknowledge had any show of defeating them.

The year 1879, in addition, saw the formulation and adoption of what has been called "the pillar of professional baseball"—the first reserve rule, by means of which each club in the League was enabled to reserve five players from its current squad for the following season's competition. The significance of this reserve privilege was that each club, henceforth, could definitely count on another year's services of at least the five best men on its team. This automatically provided each club with the nucleus of a potentially winning nine and, in turn, greatly reduced the problems previously created by players "revolving" from team to team at the end of each season.

The move to introduce greater stability in the sport was further implemented in 1880 when the League constitution was amended to empower the various clubs to suspend players without pay for gross conduct and violation of the rules.

Carrying the reform drive beyond this, the League, in September 1881, decided to create a blacklist of certain individuals "against whom the charges of general dissipation and insubordination have been repeatedly made," the intent being that "no League club should play against any club employing as manager, umpire, or player any of such proscribed players." It was also decided that reinstatement could be achieved only by a unanimous vote taken by the League membership at its annual meeting. On the first blacklist were the following nine men: M. J. Dorgan, L. P. Dickerson, E. M. Gross, L. Pike, S. P. Houk, E. Nolan, W. Crowley, J. Fox, and L. P. Brown.

It is known that the plan for creating a blacklist of undesirable athletes had been under consideration by the League for some years, but what finally precipitated the overt move may have been a series of occurrences throughout the 1881 season that reflected unfavorably on the national pastime. These events included the exposure of attempts to bribe the captain of the Cleveland baseball club to win or lose games for gamblers; the arrest and jailing of at least one ball player for running out on a room-and-board bill without payment (a common practice of many ballplayers at the time); critical editorials in influential newspapers; and sundry published news items describing unsportsmanlike displays on the ball field.

A typical editorial attack, for instance, is the one printed by *The New York Times* on August 30, which read as follows:

> There is really reason to believe that base-ball is gradually dying out in this country . . . the records of our hospitals confirm the theory that fewer games of base-ball have been played during the past year than were played during any other single year since 1868 . . . It is estimated by an able statistician that the annual number of accidents caused by base-ball in the last ten years has been 37,518, of which 3 per cent. have been fatal; 25,611 fingers and 11,016 legs were broken during the decade in question, while 1,900 eyes were permanently put out and 1,648 ribs were fractured. Had not the popularity of the game begun to decline some two years ago it would undoubtedly have been demanded by Western Democrats that base-ball cripples should be pensioned by the Government, a measure which would at once bankrupt our national Treasury.

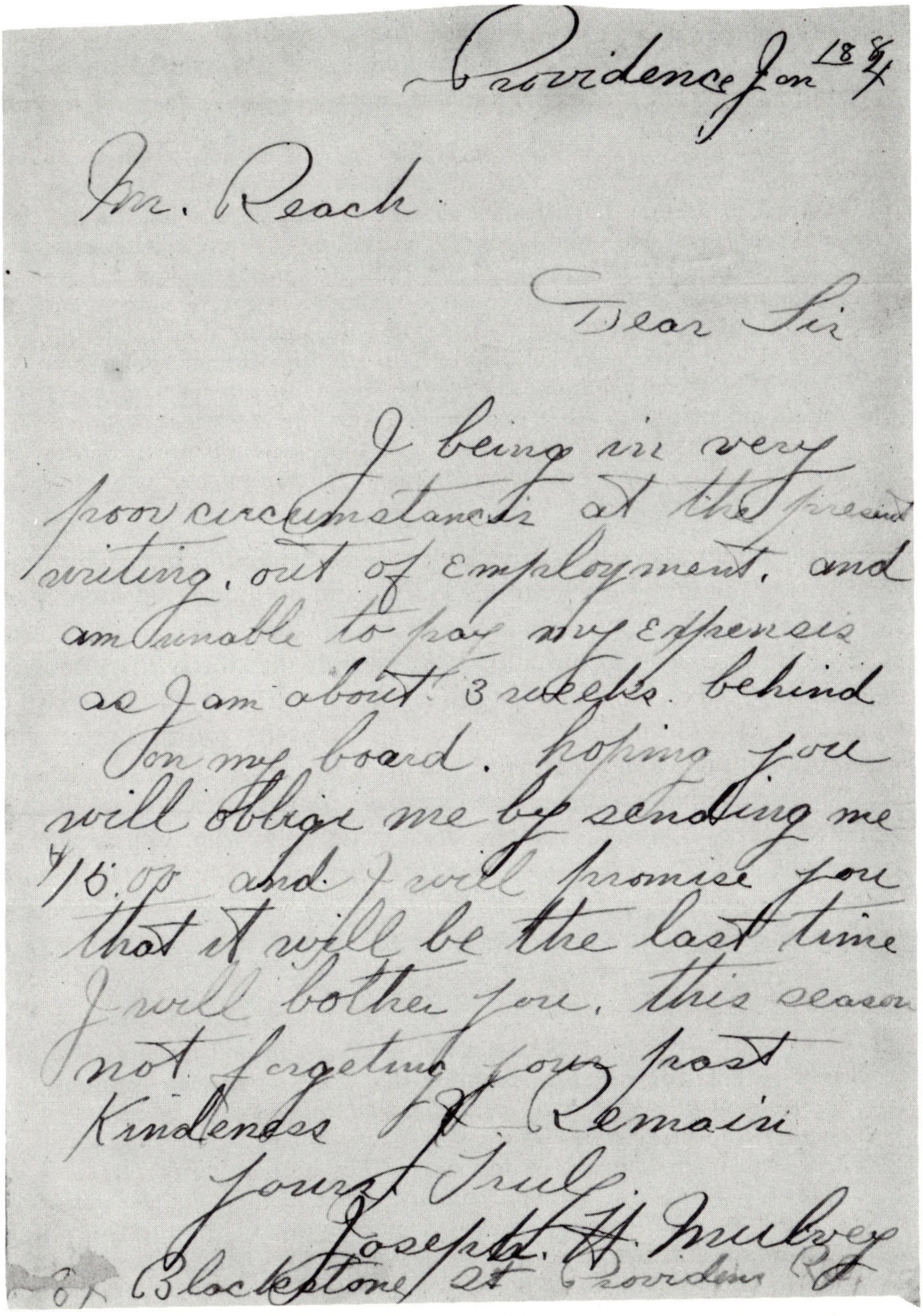

Providence Jan 18 8/4

Mr. Reach

Dear Sir

I being in very poor circumstances at the present writing, out of Employment, and am unable to pay my Expenses as I am about 3 weeks behind on my board. hoping you will oblige me by sending me $15.00 and I will promise you that it will be the last time I will bother you, this season not forgeting your past Kindeness I Remain

Yours Truly.

Joseph H Mulvey

6 Blackstone St Providence R I

JOE MULVEY covered third base for the Philadelphia Nationals over the greater part of the '8os. Like many a ballplayer of the period, he was often in financial straits, as indicated by the letter above

Typical of the damaging news item is the Buffalo *Express* account of the game between the Cleveland and Buffalo clubs, which was won by Buffalo, 8 to 5. The dispatch, dated August 31, 1881, read as follows:

> The Clevelands played their last game of the season in this city yesterday, and that they come no more is not a matter of serious regret . . . It may have been the weather, but all the men in the field seemed in the ugliest possible mood . . . The crowd, likewise, suffered from the heat, and no San Francisco hoodlums could have made a worse showing, on the same ground. Their actions were far more suited to a prize ring than a ball field, and no doubt many of them would have been far nearer home in the former. But when players set a bad example, the rough element in the spectators will follow, no matter to what extreme it leads . . . Yesterday's contest was one of heavy hitting . . . but . . . there was too much of the hoodlum about the whole game to make the hitting business even ordinarily interesting.

Even William A. Hulbert himself, the reform-minded League president, was not immune from various journalistic potshots. One such attack occurred in his own home town about six months before his death, in April 1882. In a sense, it is illuminating because it demonstrates that the man, in addition to his elevated and determined character, also was possessed of human frailty—specifically, in this case, a capacity for making glaring errors in both taste and judgment.

The particular circumstances were connected with the death and burial of United States President James A. Garfield, who was shot by an assassin on July 2 and who died on September 19, 1881. The criticism of Hulbert, whose name was deliberately misspelled, was made by the Chicago *Tribune;* and the nature and content of the item is self-explanatory.

Said the *Tribune:*

> The people of Chicago learned with mortification and disgust from the dispatches of yesterday morning that a base ball club claiming to represent this city had been engaging in a public game with another club in Troy during the very hours when the lamented Garfield was being carried to his grave. The responsibility for this shameful spectacle rests mainly upon the President of the club and of the Base Ball League, a person named Hurlbert, who must have been aware that the game was to take place, and had the power to stop it, but declined to do so. The players, however, shared in the disgrace. If any or all of them had had a spark of sensibility he or

they would have refused absolutely to celebrate the day in a manner so inappropriate.

As an additional gesture of disdain, the newspaper notified its Worcester correspondent not to report the Chicago-Worcester contests of that week, thereby temporarily withdrawing its recognition of the team as a representative of Chicago.

Nevertheless, considering the overall picture, the fact remains that Hulbert did aim high in his dedication to the reform and advancement of the national pastime, and for this and his accomplishments, baseball is in his debt.

Indeed, after Hulbert's death, a series of crises hit the sport one after another. Toward the end of May 1882, for instance, the Cleveland and Buffalo baseball clubs met in Buffalo for a series of games; once again, as in their final game of the previous season, poor sportsmanship dominated the proceedings. This is how the Buffalo *Courier* reported the story on May 27:

The Cleveland bullies shook the dust of Buffalo from their big feet last night and departed a sadder if not a wiser lot of men. They leave behind them an odium which will last as long as Buffalo people take an interest in base ball. To say that their conduct as a body has been disgraceful since their arrival here is putting it mild. On Thursday Dunlap, who is the biggest toad in the puddle, made a sorry exhibition of himself and at once fell into disfavor. The same individual, assisted by Glasscock, on Friday pitched into everybody and everything and disgusted the assemblage by their abuse of the umpire and several of the Buffalo players. But yesterday's conduct capped the climax. Dunlap, Glasscock, Shaffer and Esterbrook showed themselves to be rowdies of a low order and men totally unfit to be allowed upon a ball field. They used disgraceful language throughout the whole game, and Esterbrook demonstrated that he was a man deficient in honor and common decency. In the sixth inning Muldoon made a hit, and Esterbrook followed with a short hit to Force, which that worthy fumbled and finally recovered, but threw low to Brouthers, who in attempting to pick up the ball fell down, with Esterbrook underneath him. Muldoon started for third base, but had the Buffalo first base man been allowed to rise he could have thrown him out. As he was getting up Esterbrook put one arm and leg over Jumbo and held him down and the runner got to his base . . . Such a low, despicable action was never seen here before, and we hope never will be again. Manager O'Rourke at once put in a protest, and Hickey [the umpire] very rightly sent Muldoon back to second base, but did nothing with Esterbrook. The rule regarding such cases is very strict, and provides that the guilty party shall be declared out and be liable to a heavy fine. The crowd blamed Hickey very much for not showing his authority, and it will benefit him greatly if he will carefully study the rules in reference to fining players. The least said of Esterbrook the better. He is not only a disgrace to the League, but also to the Cleveland club, if such a thing be possible . . .

Apart from the generally negative impression derived from the antics described, what emerges from the *Courier* account is the pastime's glaring need for respected, impartial baseball authorities to govern and supervise each game—namely, good umpires.

This need was underscored time and time again, but perhaps never with as much irony as when Federal Judge Kenesaw M. Landis said, "I wouldn't umpire a baseball game for the world; it requires too much judicial and temperamental balance." The irony stems not only from the fact that the words came from one of the most eminently qualified jurists of the time, but also from the fact that the man who uttered them did so at least a decade before he became professional baseball's first all-powerful "umpire"—the first commissioner of Baseball.

Considering the power and prestige enjoyed by today's arbiters of baseball contests, the umpire's lot in the latter part of the last century was decidedly mean and inferior by comparison. Some of the reasons for this were discussed in a most informative article printed in the Chicago *Tribune*, July 30, 1882; here is what it said:

For the most part the umpires of to-day [1882] are played-out ball-tossers, fellows who are driven by necessity to accept the pittance of $5 per game which is allotted as their compensation. Instead of being, as he should be, far above the level of the ball-player, the umpire of to-day is far below that level, and properly belongs in the "bum" category. He travels, sleeps, eats, associates with the players, and frequently joins them in tossing the ball about before the game begins. It is quite likely he is when at home the associate of thieves and gamblers—at least one such case has been developed this season—and when on his travels naturally spends his leisure hours in the same company. His intimacy with players off the ballfield renders it impossible for him to be strict and impartial during a game, and a desire to curry favor with the club management which chooses him will inevitably cause him to show favor to one side or the other. Granting that he is not dishonest—which is granting a great deal in the light of developments and appearances—the average league umpire is a worthless loafer easily tempted and swayed by improper considerations, and is a very unsafe and eminently unworthy person in whose hands to place the arbitration of a game of ball played in the presence of great crowds of ladies and gentlemen.

The "case" referred to in the article above was that of Richard "Dick" Higham, whose name was removed from the list of League umpires on June 25 for having conspired with gamblers to render decisions on the ball field according to the way bets were made on the games. Higham's case, however, is the only one of its kind on record, so far as umpires are concerned.

With regard to the other facts, the situation was often even further complicated by the peculiar personalities of the umpires themselves. For example, consider the case of George Burnham, who was released as a League umpire upon the complaint of four clubs—Chicago, Detroit, Buffalo, and Boston.

Displaying a certain flair for public relations, if not sound judgment, Burnham purchased a watch for 45 dollars, and had it engraved as follows: "Presented to George W. Burnham, July 25, 1883, by his Cleveland friends." Then, he arranged to have the watch delivered by messenger to Frank Bancroft, manager of the Cleveland team, who was to ceremoniously present it to Burnham on the field at the close of the seventh inning of the game of that date.

Unfortunately for poor George, when the watch was delivered, Bancroft, suspecting a ruse, declined to make the presentation. Instead, he had the package sent to the locker room, where Burnham found it after the game.

Realizing that his scheme had backfired, Burnham decided to make the most of the situation. With much ado, he opened the package and "discovered" the watch. With real tears in his eyes and with quivering voice, he then said, "God bless the people of Cleveland. This shows that I have *some* friends left!"

The entire hoax came to light shortly thereafter when a reporter for the Cleveland *Herald*, following up on the story, investigated the matter and discovered the actual facts.

An anonymous balladeer, so affected by the tale, composed the following:

THE BALLAD OF BURNHAM

Burnham had a little watch;
    Its face was white as snow,
And everywhere that Burnham went
    The watch was sure to go.

It followed him to Cleveland once;
    It was against the rules;
It made the Providence team mad,
    And so they kicked like mules.

"What makes Cleveland love Burnham so?"
    Bold Harry Wright's men cry.
"Oh, Burnham umpires square, you know!"
    The *Herald* did reply.

For ruffianly Chicago acts
    We want to make amends;
So, noble umpire, wear this watch—
    "The gift of Cleveland friends."

But when the league turned Burnham out,
    It made the people roar
To find that Burnham bought the watch
    At a second-handed store.

The moral is so obvious
    That here the story ends
Of Burnham and his little watch—
    "The gift of Cleveland friends."

Later, still another "poet," intrigued by umpires in general, dashed off a lengthy philosophical opus concerning the species, the first two stanzas of which read:

Of all the inscrutable creatures there be
A top of the earth or below in the sea,
The ump is the beatenest being, sure. He
Consorteth apart in mystery.

His integument's blue, there's a pad on his chest,
His frontal is masked and his features unguessed;
On his mind is a cap, and—well, as for the rest
Whatever it be, it's the subject of jest.

And "the subject of jest" indeed the umpire was. Jokes and jibes abounded; for example:

When a man sinks so low that he no longer has a friend on earth, the position of base ball umpire is all that is left him.

This country will never lack brave and reckless men so long as there are so many of them willing to act as base ball umpires.

"Papa," said a small boy not well posted on base ball, "what does the umpire do?" "He does pretty much as he pleases, my son," replied the father, who had studied the game very carefully.

One way of snatching victory from defeat is to mob the base ball umpire.

Frequently, of course—and with certain justification—the umpires themselves could not quite see the humor involved, especially in situations where they were to be made the butt of mob action. A case in point—in fact, one in which the "worm" actually turned—occurred in Philadelphia in the spring of 1884. During a game between the Philadelphia Club and the Athletic Club, the umpire, a man named McLean, became so riled at the crowd's mockery that he picked up a bat, walked to the fence in right field, and hurled it up among the spectators.

When the bat struck an innocent man, the crowd became so enraged that they tried to storm the playing field to get at the umpire. Fortunately for McLean, swift police intervention saved him from a lynching, but not from arrest at the end of the game. A howling mob followed the arresting officer and the umpire all the way to the police station.

On May 12, 1884, recognizing—perhaps somewhat belatedly—the very significant role that the press in particular had played in such affairs, by consciously and unconsciously engendering disrespect for baseball umpires over the years, the Philadelphia *Item* printed the following:

Men capable of satisfactorily filling the important position of umpire are few, and those who are competent are often deterred from accepting the position on account of the abuse showered on them by the papers. Philadelphia, we are sorry to say, is among the worst of cities for abusing umpires, and in this abuse the newspapers take the lead. It is the comments of the papers that excite the crowd, and after that, whether right or wrong, the umpire comes in for plenty of abuse. To comment fairly on an umpire's decision is perfectly legitimate; to abuse him is all wrong. *The Item* proposes always to sustain umpires when they show a spirit of honesty, but when it is evident that their rulings are for dishonest ends, we shall be among the first to condemn. The press can do more to have honest and satisfactory umpiring than any other means that could be employed. It can do this by temperate criticism, not by abuse. Let the press try it once, and see if *The Item* is not right.

In any event, to improve the situation, the League, some months earlier had engaged the services of several professional umpires at specified annual salaries. And to ensure their impartiality, the men were selected from cities that were not represented in the League.

Actually, the move to hire regular umpires was preceded by, and made in emulation of, a similar action taken the year before by the American Association, a new professional circuit, organized in November of 1881. The American Association represented the first real challenge to the National League's pre-eminence on the professional baseball scene; and the challenge was offered on several different levels, among which were the following:

League clubs charged fifty cents for admission to games; Association clubs, twenty-five cents.

League clubs did not play on Sunday; Association clubs did.

Sale of intoxicating beverages was prohibited in League parks; beer was sold in Association parks.

As is evident, the differences listed above were geared mainly to the attraction of spectators away from the games of one circuit, to attendance at those of the other. However, a much more serious problem was the one posed to the pastime itself by the talent raids of Association clubs on League clubs, and vice versa. Since it was not bound by League laws, "reserved" players, suspended players, and those on the official blacklist, were all fair game for the Association; and a sort of baseball "war" ensued with each organization trying either to retain or to pirate players from the other.

In 1883, both circuits recognized the folly of a suicidal struggle of this sort, and together with the Northwestern League, a minor circuit, they entered into the historic peace pact known as the Tripartite Agreement, later called the National Agreement.

According to this instrument, each organization pledged itself to recognize and respect the laws and contracts of the other two. For example, a vital section of the Agreement stated:

> When a player under contract by any club . . . is expelled, black-listed, or suspended, in accordance with its rules . . . notice of such disqualification shall be served upon the Secretaries of the other associations . . . and upon the receipt of such notice, all club members of all the parties hereto shall be debarred from employing or playing with or against such disqualified player, until the period of disqualification shall have terminated, *or the disqualification be revoked by the association from which such player was disqualified.*

In simple language, this meant that any professional player who broke his club contract would automatically find himself unemployed; for under the terms of the accord, no other professional club would hire him.

In addition, among various other provisions, the Agreement gave to each club in both major circuits the privilege of reserving eleven players instead of the previous five, thus providing each franchised member with more than a full team's complement of men for the subsequent season's competition.

But peace was not destined to prevail so easily. By the end of 1883, a new baseball crisis was brewing; and by 1884, it had blown itself into a full-fledged storm, for by then, still another professional circuit had been formed—the Union Association.

The UA was essentially the personal venture of Henry V. Lucas, a so-called millionaire "crank" from St. Louis who believed he saw an opportunity of making additional millions through the renewed popularity of the national pastime. If two major circuits were flourishing, reasoned Lucas, why not three? Using the old lures of more money and better conditions, and posing as a champion of the "exploited" players who were bound to their contracts by unfair "reserve" clauses, he succeeded in setting up a third major circuit despite the combined efforts of the National League and the American Association to stave him off.

But now, as had happened so many times in the past, public reaction set in again. Conflicting game schedules, player piracy, "reserve"-jumping, contract-breaking, etc., all contributed to a great and sudden drop in attendance at the various professional ball parks. Unable to survive the financial strain thus imposed, the Union Association collapsed at the end of 1884 and disbanded in January of 1885.

Commenting on the demise of the UA, the Cleveland *Herald*, of January 16, said:

> It has enacted no new laws, brought out no valuable players, and leaves not one piece of healthy legislation on its annals. It has caused several players to be cast out of the ranks of reputable professionals and has given a few others a chance to show the treachery that was in them. Thus, accidentally, it may have rendered the National group of clubs a service, but no credit is to be given for the service. The result has been predicted in these columns and its coming so soon is gratifying. All reputable players and managers are to be congratulated on it.

Nevertheless, Henry V. Lucas, the UA's originator, did not completely disappear from the baseball scene together with the Association. For, in some very skillful negotiations, Lucas had managed to extract from the National League the promise of a club franchise in the city of St. Louis. This he received despite the strong opposition of League President Abraham G. Mills, who resigned in protest over the matter.

With Mills's departure, Nicholas E. Young assumed the leadership of the League; thus, slowly, another baseball crisis subsided.

TEN

BIZARRE BASEBALL—
A NINETEENTH CENTURY
CRAZE

In the years after the Civil War and through the period of Reconstruction, the nation—as has been noted—was seized with a growing interest in athletics and physical exercise. This development was called variously "athleticism," "the athletic craze," "sporting fever," etc.; it continued to manifest itself right into the twentieth century.

However, the craze known specifically as "baseball fever" reached a curious and interesting plateau in the decade of the eighties.

The resurgence of the professional game and the formation of major new baseball circuits were aspects of the phenomenon. This extended to the various colleges and universities of the nation, where the sport also was flourishing on an amateur level. Throughout the land, hundreds of teams were competing in dozens of local minor leagues, some of which included the following: Northwestern, Eastern, New England, Eastern New England, Western, Southern, Central Pennsylvania, Ohio State, California State, etc.

Baseball had even bridged the gap of national boundaries and was being played by Canadians and Americans in the International League,

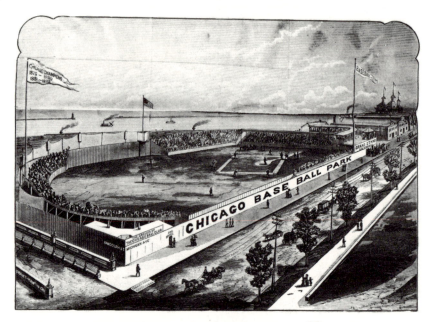

THE NEW CHICAGO BASE BALL PARK, 1883,
where, "including standing room, an attendance of fully 10,000 people can be cared for."

which was organized in 1886. In addition, it was being introduced in Cuba, England, France, Australia, Japan, and various other foreign lands.

Of course, the United States remained the hotbed of the sport; here, various odd experiments and developments were taking place. Around 1880, for instance—unlikely as it may seem—two baseball teams were organized in Albany, New York, to play the game regularly off Boston and Albany Islands in the waters of the Hudson River! The pitcher, catcher, and batter all stood in water up to their waist; the fielders floated, swam, or stood about in the river, whichever alternative was most feasible.

In Buffalo, New York, in 1882, a series of games were played between teams of so-called "Phats" and "Leans," which attracted among the spectators such prominent personages as the mayor of the city, many city-hall officials, and nearly all the members of the common council.

The "Phats" were made up of players weighing a minimum of 200 pounds each, and the "Leans," a maximum of 140 pounds each. John Wander, the "Phat" first baseman, tilted the scales at 260 pounds; J. Ferguson, the "Lean" center fielder, registered a mere 110 pounds. Total weight of the fatties was 1,904 pounds; that of the skinnies, 1,081 pounds.

By 1883, baseball fever was running so high in Philadelphia, that a group called the Snorkey Base-ball Club was organized to play an outfit named the Hoppers. What made these teams unique was that the Snorkeys consisted entirely of one-armed athletes, and the Hoppers, of men who had each lost a leg!

The teams practiced and played regularly in the city of brotherly love; and they attracted a good deal of attention not only because of the nature of the teams but also because some of the players had been expert athletes before having become disabled.

In New York, that same season, the fever reached such odd proportions that the New York Metropolitans signed the famous heavyweight prizefighter John L. Sullivan to pitch for them as a star attraction.

This is how *The New York Times*, on May 29, 1883, reported the great John L's debut on the diamond:

> For 50 per cent. of the gate money Mr. John L. Sullivan, Boston's pet pugilist, consented to play before a New-York audience as pitcher in a base-ball nine. The exhibition took place on the Polo Grounds yesterday afternoon, and fully 4,000 persons assembled to witness it. The price of admission to the grand stand was doubled, but this did not prevent its being comfortably filled. Such decorum was observed by its male occupants that the sprinkling of ladies seemed not at all out of place. The element that contributed the worshipers and friends of Mr. Sullivan found seats outside the grand stand. A tally-ho, half a dozen hacks, some light carriages, and a butcher's cart or two composed the assemblage of vehicles skirting the edge of the ball-field. For the two hours and nineteen minutes which Mr. Sullivan labored as a ball-player he probably received about $1,200. The game was between the Metropolitan nine, with whom Mr. Sullivan served as pitcher, and a picked nine. The game throughout was anything but brilliant, and but for Mr. Sullivan's presence would have flattened out completely. "How long since you have handled a ball?" was asked the pugilist. "Six years. I used to play pitcher and catcher in Boston with the Emmets and Tremonts," was the reply. Mr. Sullivan appeared in a white flannel suit, with blue stockings and a white cap, his banged black hair showing to good advantage beneath its turned up peak. A blue shield was inworked upon the left arm from the shoulder down. His breadth of shoulder, thick legs, and expansive rump distinguished him from every other player in the field. Whenever he took his place at the pitcher's plate or at the bat the spectators craned their necks and watched every movement that he made. As a ball-tosser, Mr. Sullivan's ability was gauged exactly by the boy who remarked, disgustedly, "No good" . . .

THREE STUDIES OF JOHN L. AS A BASEBALL PITCHER
As seen by Homer C. Davenport, in a game between
the Ironsides of Newark and the Weehawken team of West New York.

A quarter of a century later, the fabled fighter revealed, in his characteristically "modest" manner, the actual amount of money he had earned on the ball field:

> They talk about the heavy salaries that are paid to players, but the fact remains that I have the best average ever made, so far as the salary paid me . . . How does $2,200 for one game strike you? Well, I received that bunch of money for my services as umpire in a game on the old Polo grounds in the early eighties, umpiring for Jim Mutrie and the Metropolitans . . . (and, as a pitcher) I made some $8,000 in four games, which was going some.

The growing taste for bizarre baseball in the 1880s could hardly have been expected to continue for long without escaping the attention of the great journals and press of the period. Consequently, on June 9, 1883, *Harper's Weekly*, as a tongue-in-cheek commentary, published a large illustration of a baseball game being played on horseback! This was accompanied by the following tart remarks:

BASEBALL OF THE FUTURE.

Already the season has produced several novelties in the base-ball line. A game has been played by electric light in the West.* In Philadelphia a contest between a two-legged, one-armed nine and a two-armed, one-legged nine resulted in a victory for the former, who now claim the cripple championship of the world. A nine composed of colored women is nearly ready to enter the field. In this city a club has greatly increased its gate receipts by putting a famous pugilist on exhibition as pitcher. This idea might be carried farther. A nine made up of the wild Australian children as the battery, the transparent-headed baby as short stop, Zulus on the bases, and bearded women and living skeletons in the field, would go far toward satisfying even the strongest craving for novelty.

Lest it be thought that this "craving for novelty" in baseball was unique only to the eighties, consider the game played in Hoboken on September 21, 1861, barely six months after the start of the Civil War.

The contest involved nine picked players on one side and eighteen on the other side. Half of the eighteen-man team were cricketers, while the remainder were first-nine players chosen from among the leading amateur clubs of the time, including the Mutuals.

* The incandescent lamp had been invented by Thomas Alva Edison only four years earlier, in 1879; and the game referred to here is one of the first—if not the very first—ever to have been played under lights. The contest took place in Fort Wayne, Indiana, on June 2, between the home team and a nine from Quincy, Illinois. Fort Wayne was the victor, in seven innings, by the score of 19 runs to 11.

In addition, because of its size, the eighteen-man team was allowed six outs to an inning, instead of the usual three. Yet, despite this advantage and their numerical superiority on the field, the larger team lost by a score of 45 to 16.

The explanation, of course, lay in the fact that the fabulous Jim Creighton, using his puzzling low-wrist-throw delivery, was pitching for the winners. Creighton, although still a youth, had become a baseball legend in his own brief lifetime. A most versatile player, it was he who triggered one of the first triple plays in baseball. The occasion was a match game, played on July 22, 1860, between the Brooklyn Excelsiors and the Baltimore Excelsiors. With men on second and third, and none out, Creighton, who was playing left field at the time, made a spectacular one-handed catch of the batter's long fly for the first out. With a swift throw to the third baseman, who in turn relayed the ball to second, he caught both runners off base, and the triple play was accomplished.

When Creighton died in 1862, the Excelsior Club, for whom he had pitched so many notable games, erected a large granite monument over his grave, which is located in Greenwood Cemetery, Brooklyn. Carved on the face of the granite and encircled by a wreath is a design featuring a pair of crossed bats, a scorebook, a base, and a baseball cap. Above is a scroll bearing the single word "Excelsior"; below, the words "James Creighton, son of James and Jane Creighton, April 15, 1841; October 18, 1862"; and balanced on the very summit of the granite column, there rests a stone baseball.

The *Brooklyn Eagle,* in its obituary of October 20, 1862, said the following:

> The remains of the late James P. Creighton, familiar in Base Ball and cricket circles as one of the best players in the Union, were yesterday conveyed to their last resting place, followed by a large number of friends and relatives.
>
> The circumstances of his death are very touching. In the late match with the Unions (Tuesday last) the deceased sustained an internal injury occasioned by strain while batting. After suffering for a few days, he expired on Saturday afternoon last at the residence of his father, 307 Henry Street. The remains were encased in a handsome rosewood coffin, with silver mountings, and upon a silver plate was inscribed the name, age, etc., of the deceased— "James P. Creighton, 21 years, 7 months and 2 days."

So was baseball's first tragic hero buried.

But now, two decades later, the sport was in the throes of one extravagant performance after another. Even the writers of baseball news were vying with each other in the press for novel forms of expression. Witness the headline over a *Special Dispatch to the Herald,* dated "Buffalo, N. Y., May 12, 1883," which read as follows:

SOUNDS FROM THE FIELD

—

**Oh, List to the Foul and the
Umpire's Howl,**

—

**The Whirr of the Bat When
It Goes Through the Air,**

—

**And the Buzz of the Fly as It
Speeds Here and There.**

—

LEAGUE CONFLICTS

—

Then, on August 19, 1883, *The New York Times* reported "A Ridiculous Exhibition at a Philadelphia Park"—which was nothing more nor less than a baseball game played between two teams of girls!

Considering the period, such an event was a relatively rare phenomenon, and two days later, the newspaper devoted a good deal of editorial space to the contest. This is what it said:

> The game of Base-ball recently played in Philadelphia by gorgeously dressed young women was confessedly a failure, and it established the fact that base-ball, unlike the modern drama, cannot be made exclusively an exhibition of clothing . . . The base-ball girls had undoubtedly been trained with great care . . . When, however, the girls played in public . . . they did not cover themselves with glory—much as they stood in need of some kind of covering. With the exception of a mouse, there is probably nothing more dangerous than a baseball flying through the air directly at some unprotected girl. Such, at least, was the opinion of the ball-playing girls. The batter alone showed no signs of fear, for there was, of course, no probability that the balls aimed at her would come near her. The other players, whenever a ball came in their direction, would exclaim loudly, "Oh, my!" and would

Montage of old-time sports writers.

frantically dodge it. No casualties either among the girls or the spectators occurred, for the reason that no girl was able to throw the ball swiftly enough to inflict a severe blow. Still, had it hit a girl in the eye or on the back hair it might have caused some inconvenience. Of course, the girls did not venture to catch the ball. They could not have caught it had they tried, for the simple reason that they were standing on their feet and were without aprons. To expect a girl in such circumstances to catch a ball would be absurd . . . After all, it is very doubtful if girls can be made efficient base-ball players. They can far surpass the male "Red Stockings" and "White Stockings" in the splendor of their costumes, but in all probability the sacred cause of art would suffer less were they to display their clothes on the stage instead of the ball field.

As might have been expected, the editorial served only to publicize the idea of girls' games; and New York City, not to be outdone by Philadelphia in any respect, staged a comparable contest about a month later, which the newspaper called, "A Base-Ball Burlesque."

Describing the actual event, the *Times* said:

A crowd of about 1,500 people assembled on the Manhattan Athletic Club's grounds, at Eighty-sixth-street and Eighth-avenue, yesterday afternoon, and laughed themselves hungry and thirsty watching a game of base-ball between two teams composed of girls . . . One side was composed of brunettes, whose costumes were of an irritating red; the other was of blondes who wore sympathetic blue . . . The costumes were bathing dresses of the ancient and honorable order. The loose body had a long, flowing skirt, which reached below the knee. Stockings of the regulation style, base-ball shoes, and white hats completed the outfit . . . These young ladies, as the management of the affair announced, were selected withe tender solicitude from 200 applicants, variety actresses and ballet girls being positively barred. Only three of the lot had ever been on the stage, and they were in the strictly legitimate business. One of them, Miss Daisy Muir, short stop for the blondes, once played Eva in "Uncle Tom's Cabin," and also once won a prize offered by a Philadelphia paper for the best reply to an offer of marriage. Most of the others were graduates of Sunday-schools and normal colleges, who had seen the vanity of Greek and Latin and yearned to emulate the examples of the great and good students of Yale, Harvard, and Princeton by traveling wholly on their muscle. They were of assorted sizes and shapes. Some were short and stout, some were tall and thin; others were short and thin, and still others tall and stout. They played base-ball in a very sad and sorrowful sort of way, as if the vagaries of the ball had been too great for their struggling intellects . . . Base-ball was not what it was painted, and they were evidently sighing for the end of the season . . . Toward the end of the game the girls began to show symptoms of sadness and weariness, and doggedly refused to run from one base to another, until it became morally certain that the other side was hopelessly tangled up with the ball. Often, when the fielders could not stop the ball in any other way they sat down on it. This was at once effective and picturesque, and never missed gaining a howl of applause . . . When five innings had been played, and the back hair and brains of the girls appeared to be in a hopelessly demoralized condition, with a tendency on the part of their hose to follow suit, the game was called . . . The score was 54 to 22 . . . in favor of the brunettes. They play again tomorrow.

Actually, these particular contests were not the first of their kind. Back in 1875, two all-girl teams—also called the "Blondes" and "Brunettes"—played baseball publicly in the cities of Springfield and Decatur, Illinois. The Western girls, however, appear to have placed more emphasis on the game rather than on their costumes, for their uniforms, although described as "handsome" and "new," did not differ materially from those worn by ordinary clubs.

Nevertheless, since these rare girls' games were played primarily for money, they may best be regarded as more or less inept public spectacles, rather than true sporting events.

And yet, during the same period, there were still other girls who played the game in earnest, for the fun and exercise to be derived therefrom. Their games, however, were played in secret.

Sophia F. Richardson, a Vassar College girl, revealed some of this in a paper entitled "Tendencies in Athletics for Women," presented in 1896 to the Association of Collegiate Alumnae. This is what she said:

About twenty years ago [1876], when I was a freshman, seven or eight baseball clubs suddenly came into being, spontaneously as it seemed, but I think they owed their existence to a few quiet suggestions from a resident physician, wise beyond her generation. The public, so far as it knew of our playing, was shocked, but in our retired grounds, and protected from observation even in these grounds by sheltering trees, we continued to play in spite of a censorious public. One day a student, while running between bases, fell, with an injured leg. We attended her to the infirmary, with the foreboding that this accident would end our play of baseball. Not so. Dr. Webster said that the public doubtless would condemn the game as too violent, but that if the student had hurt herself while dancing the public would not condemn dancing to extinction. Singular point was given to her remark a few days later, when a student did fall while dancing and broke her leg. After this we played with the feeling somewhat lightened that we were enjoying delightful but contraband pleasure. The interest in baseball did not increase; clubs were not formed by incoming classes. I think there was too much pressure against it from disapproving mothers. However, those of us who had learned the value of vigorous play succeeded in keeping alive enough interest in the game to support two clubs until our senior year.

But if public opinion frowned on the active and serious participation of girls in the national pastime, it certainly was not averse to having members of the fair sex bestow their presence as spectators at contests between teams of men. Indeed, this tradition dated all the way back to the early match games of the Knickerbocker, Gotham, and other gentlemen's baseball clubs, played at the Elysian Fields in Hoboken and elsewhere.

In fact, with the rise of professional baseball, many clubs welcomed the presence of ladies at the contests to lend an air of gentility to the proceedings, which frequently tended to get out of hand. And to further encourage female attendance at the professional ball parks, the institution known as "Ladies' Day" came into being.

Ladies Day, as is commonly known, is simply a day set aside during the week on which ladies are admitted free of charge to the ball park or, in some cases, at a reduced rate to the grand stand.

The Brooklyn Club was one of the very first to inaugurate this custom, in 1884, although other Ladies Days are known to have been scheduled by smaller baseball clubs before that date. An anonymous commentator of the time discussed the matter in this vein:

> Nothing is so well calculated to popularize the national game of the country among the best classes of the community as the encouragement of the presence of ladies at the matches . . . To realize the advantage of the attendance of the fair sex at matches it is only necessary to contrast the behavior of a large crowd of spectators at a ball match during an exciting contest when no ladies are present with that of an assemblage in which are to be seen hundreds of bright-eyed fair ones occupying seats on the grand stand. At the former, profanity, ill feeling, partisan prejudice and other characteristics of "stag" gatherings are conspicuous features, while at the other the pride of gentlemen which curbs men's evil passions in the presence of ladies frowns upon all such exhibitions of partisan ill will, and order and decorum mark the presence of the civilizing influence of the fair sex.

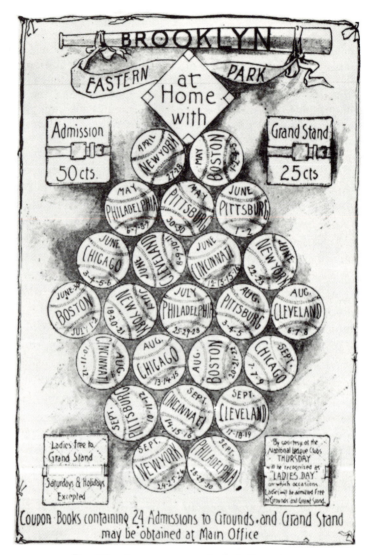

Brooklyn home game schedule for 1890.
Note the "Ladies Day" announcements at the bottom

And the fair sex, in ever-increasing numbers, did come out of their homes, nurseries, factories, and offices to grace the baseball parks with their presence. That 1885 was witnessing one of the most exciting professional races in years also provided additional stimulus to female interest and attendance.

Sitting on the grand stand at the Polo Grounds on any fair day in the baseball season one may see hundreds of pretty ladies deeply interested in the work of the Giants and their opponents. Many of them know nothing of the science of the game, and insist on applauding at the wrong time; others get greatly excited and behave so one minute that they blush with shame the next, and still others know all the fine points and can score as well as any man and better than a majority of the male attendants at a game. Among the latter are Mrs. John Montgomery Ward, the pretty wife of New York's short stop, and her sister, Mrs. Helm. Mrs. Ward was, before her marriage to the Giants' infielder, Miss Helen Dauvray. She has long been interested in baseball, and last year gave for competition the "Dauvray Cup" and medals which were won by the Detroit team. Mrs. Ward is a

HELEN DAUVRAY WARD. regular attendant at the Polo grounds, and usually occupies a seat on the right wing of the ladies' pavilion. She sat there Thursday when THE WORLD'S artist made brave to take her portrait. Pretty and petite, Mrs. Ward would command attention anywhere. She has a most fascinating manner and is most cool and collected un-

MRS. JOHN MONTGOMERY WARD
Wife of New York's short stop
"a regular attendant at the Polo Grounds."

STEPHEN A. BRADY
Outfielder for Mets, 1883-1886
Cover of score card, 1886

By the end of July, for instance, Chicago and New York were the leading contenders for the National League championship, Chicago having won 53 games and lost 14, while New York had won 50 and lost 16. The two teams met on August 1st at the Polo Grounds, before 14,000 avid fans; and this is how the New York press, on August 2nd, reported the event:

The interest in base ball has been increasing anew within the past few years, and yesterday's climax of popular excitement brought to mind the multitudes, the uproar, and the feverish interest that marked the great games on the Union and Capitoline grounds in Brooklyn almost twenty years ago. No portion of the populace is insensible to this craze . . . The ladies are regular and numerous attendants at the grounds. The hundreds of them who stood on the seats and screamed and waved their handkerchiefs and brandished their fans in ecstasies of applause yesterday knew enough to come early and avoid the crush.

WILLIAM A. SUNDAY.

How much they knew of the game, though none of them ever play it, was to be seen by the way they behaved. As they took their seats in the grand stand they brought out their score cards and pencils, argued over the merits of the coming players, and consulted little diaries, in which they had entered records of past League games. The rough and blackened finger tips of some of them showed them to be working girls; others, by unmistakable signs, even when they had not their children with them, showed that they were housewives and mothers; others still, by their costly dresses and the carriages they came in, were seen to be well-to-do women and young girls, and a few were of that class of female gamblers and sporting women that has grown so considerable in this city of late years.

All the time the women were settling themselves in their places the crush at the gates was growing. Men and boys were pouring out of the elevated depot, out of the horse cars, out of carriages and business wagons, and around the street corners to mingle with the pushing, crowding, squeezing throng at the gates. So large a crowd has never been seen at a horse race or a walking match or a boxing contest in this city. Rarely do such varying sorts of persons meet together on such equality anywhere. Bankers, merchants, professional men, and idlers from the clubs took their share of the squeezing side by side with laborers, office boys, ragamuffins, rowdies, city officials, clergymen, gamblers, and all the rest . . .

For the record, the New York nine won this particular game by the close score of 7 to 6. But Chicago went on to win the season's championship, with a total of 87 victories against 25 defeats, compared to New York's 85 wins and 27 losses.

For Chicago, and its able manager, Adrian "Cap" Anson, this represented the team's fourth pennant in six seasons. And, curiously, contributing to the team's winning ways—as well as to the team's championship effort in 1886—was a man who was destined to become in later years one of the nation's most famous evangelists, William A. Sunday, better known as "Billy" Sunday.

The "Parson," as he was affectionately called, played the outfield for Chicago from 1883 through 1887, after which time he played for both Pittsburgh and Philadelphia, respectively. When he left professional baseball, in 1891, he became active in the Chicago YMCA; in 1896, he began his evangelical career.

That he had once been a well-known professional ballplayer, of course, set him apart from other more conventional missionaries; fully aware of this, Sunday capitalized on his athletic background by cleverly interspersing baseball anecdotes in his sermons.

BILLY SUNDAY IN THE BOX.

Cartoon from "The Spectacular Career of Rev. 'Billy' Sunday"
by Theodore T. Frankenberg, 1913.

One of his favorite stories concerned the final game between Chicago
and Detroit in the hot pennant race of 1886, which was won by Chicago.
This was the way Billy told it:

> The last half of the ninth inning was being played. Two men were
> out and Detroit, with Charley Bennett at bat, had one man on second
> and another on third. He had two strikes on him and three balls
> called, when he fell on a ball with terrific force. It started for the
> clubhouse. Benches had been placed in the field for spectators and as I
> saw the ball sailing through my section of the air I realized that it was
> going over the crowd, and I called, "Get out of the way." The crowd
> opened and as I ran and leaped those benches I said one of the swiftest
> prayers that was ever offered. It was: "Lord, if you ever helped a mortal
> man, help me get that ball."
> I went over the benches as though wings were carrying me up.
> I threw out my hand while in the air and the ball struck and stuck.
> The game was ours. Though the deduction is hardly orthodox, I am
> sure the Lord helped me catch that ball, and it was my first great
> lesson in prayer.

On December 19, 1891, a seven-verse poem was printed in the pages of the *Sporting News* that can best be described—like Billy Sunday's deduction—as "hardly orthodox," yet essentially religious in character. Replete with baseball metaphors, the poem was also, in its own way, a religious "lesson," and although published anonymously, could easily have been written by "Parson" Billy Sunday himself. The verses were as follows:

His nose had been knocked a little awry,
    But his glance was straight and true,
And the three fingers left on his big right hand
    Gripped hard on the back of his pew.

And he said:—"My friend, I'm off my base
    When I stand in a box here like this,
But I feel, when the umpire says "play ball,"
    That we ought to play, hit or miss.

When we sign with the church we are expected to play
    Every day, hot or cold, rain or shine.
And I tell you, my friends, a very strong game
    Is put up by Satan's nine.

If we come to bat in the strength of the Lord
    Grip the willow for giving hard knocks,
We'll just get onto the devil's curves
    And knock him out of the box.

Sometimes we line her out for two bags,
    Steal third in most elegant state.
But get stuck on ourselves, take too many risks,
    And get nipped by old Nick at the plate.

And plenty of times when your side's about out
    You seem doomed to die on a base,
But whenever you hear our captain say "Go"
    Get away at your very best pace!

Never mind what the crowd say, go hard for home!
    Slide in on your feet! Darn the clothes!
There's an umpire above who will know if you're in,
    His judgment is right and it "goes".

Mention has already been made of those bizarre baseball clubs of Philadelphia, the Snorkeys and the Hoppers, whose stalwart members needed more than just simple faith and prayers in order to play ball— indeed, they required great pluck, courage, and determination, for the players consisted entirely of one-armed and one-legged men.

However, special mention must be made of one severely handicapped player in particular who pitched regular professional big-league baseball throughout most of the eighties—Hugh "One Arm" Daily. A reporter for the *Cleveland Herald,* on May 25, 1882, described the man as follows:

> He is a swarthy and by no means good-looking fellow, his uniform of flaring green adding to his unattractiveness. But he is a good pitcher. He has been doing some excellent work for the Buffalos, his main point of strength resting in his good judgment and headwork. His infirmity naturally makes him slow in handling the ball, but while this seems to give him no concern, it troubles the batter very much, and while the man with one hand is getting ready to deliver the ball, the batsman gets nervous and all unbalanced, as it were, striking generally when he ought not to and failing to when he ought. At times Daily's delivery is very speedy, but he appears to rest most confidence in his curves and drops.

One week earlier, Daily had appeared in the box against Adrian Anson's champion Chicago team and had emerged victorious by a score of 6 to 2, giving up only six hits. "Daily is regarded as somewhat of a phenomenon" read the May 17th dispatch reporting the game from Chicago to *The Courier* in Buffalo, "his left arm being gone between the elbow and wrist, and perhaps the spectacle of a piece of a man daring to toss balls to the champions may have created consternation in their ranks. At all events they were unable to 'catch on' to his delivery, and the results were disastrous."

Interestingly, "One Arm" Daily was not the only physically handicapped athlete to have played major-league baseball. In 1945, Pete Gray, also with only one arm (the left), successfully played the outfield for the St. Louis Browns.

During the first decade of this century, Mordecai Brown, who as a youth had lost two fingers in a meat-chopping accident, achieved renown as "Three-Finger" Brown, the great curve-ball hurler of the Chicago Nationals.

And during the last decade of the last century, William "Dummy" Hoy, a deaf mute, became famous playing the outfield for at least five different major-league ball clubs.

But perhaps the most remarkable example of all of a major-leaguer's overcoming a physical handicap to play ball is that of Charles Radbourn, whose story is probably the most bizarre in baseball history. For "Old Hoss," as he came to be known, practically won the National League pennant for his team single-handedly.

The time was 1884, and Radbourn was the only regular pitcher for Providence, the other, Charles Sweeney, having defected in midseason to St. Louis of the Union Association. The Providence club was on the verge

CHARLES RADBOURN.
In 1884 he singlehandedly pitched the Providence Club into the National League championship.

ADRIAN C. ANSON
Captain of the Chicago Baseball Club.
Champion League Batter of 1879, 1881 and 1887.

of disbanding when Frank Bancroft, the team manager, was approached by one of the club directors. Bancroft himself later related the story:

> I was asked my opinion and I said that if I were given permission to do what I desired with Radbourn I believed the club could yet win the flag . . . I said, "give me a written agreement that Radbourn shall be exempt from reserve at the close of the season." This was readily agreed to. I knew that "Rad." wanted to get away from Providence owing to the fact that he could do better financially elsewhere. I showed "Rad." the agreement and he said, "I will win or pitch my right arm off." How well he fulfilled his promise is

STEAL UP

Cover of scorecard, 1886

history. Providence won 20 victories in succession and "Rad." pitched
in 18 of these games, Conley being victor in the other two. In all
Radbourn pitched in 27 consecutive games, winning 26 of them,
thus enabling Providence to win the pennant.

Actually, over the entire season of 1884, Radbourn pitched a grand
total of 72 games, winning 60 while losing only 12. In addition, he par-

TWO STRIKES

ticipated in over a dozen other games, playing at different times each of the various infield positions—first, second, third, and short—as well as the outfield. And finally, to cap his astonishing record, "Old Hoss defeated the champion New York Metropolitans of the American Association in three straight games of a postseason series.

As for Radbourn s physical handicap—what was it? The answer—a little-known fact—is that "Old Hoss" suffered from a chronically lame arm.

Manager Bancroft, paying tribute to the man a decade after his death in 1897, said:

> His showing [in 1884] was all the more remarkable and phenomenal when one knows that this great pitcher suffered untold agony in endeavoring to attain the goal for which he worked so hard and so pluckily. Morning after morning upon arising he would be unable to raise his arm high enough to use his hair brush. Instead of quitting he stuck all the harder to his task going out to the ball park hours before the rest of the team and beginning to warm up by throwing a few feet and increasing the distance until he could finally throw the ball from the outfield to the home plate. The players, all eagerness to win, would watch "Rad." and when he would succeed in making his customary long-distance throw they would look at each other and say the "Old Hoss" is ready and we can't be beat, and this proved to be the case nine times out of ten.

In 1891, Radbourn retired from baseball. His arm had grown steadily worse each season after his triumphal year, even though he still managed to average better than 20 victories a year for the intervening seven years. Proud man that he was, "Old Hoss" refused to play in the minor leagues, so he opened a billiard parlor in Bloomington, Illinois, and spent his declining years in steadily increasing obscurity, growing more and more morose with time. Finally, after suffering briefly from paresis, he died in his sixty-second year, a lonely, senile man.

ELEVEN

THE PLAYERS' LEAGUE— NATIONAL LEAGUE "WAR"

One of the curious ironies of our national pastime is that the player reserve rule, the so-called "pillar of professional baseball"—by means of which a certain basic stability first was introduced to the sport—should also have been one of the game's most disruptive influences.

When initially formulated in 1879, the reserve rule (which later was expanded and embodied in the National Agreement of 1883) enabled the various clubs to somehow cope with the serious problems arising at the beginning and end of each season from the widespread practice of many players of "revolving" from team to team for higher pay.

Then, in 1884, along came Henry V. Lucas, brashly luring "reserved" players away from both the American Association and the National League, and signing them for his new baseball circuit, the Union Association.

This was followed, late in 1885, by the formation of the professional athletes' benevolent society, known as the National Brotherhood of Baseball Players, whose three paramount aims were: "to protect and benefit its members collectively and individually; to promote a high standard of professional conduct;" and "to advance the interests of the 'National Game.'"

John Montgomery Ward, captain and crack shortstop of the New York Club, was the prime mover in the founding of the Brotherhood—which actually was accomplished in secret—and he remained a central figure in the events that led to the formation of the Players' League and, ultimately, to the National League-Players' League "war" of 1890.

But that is leaping ahead too swiftly. For the moment, let us revert to the year 1886 and John Ward describing some of his own baseball experiences in the August issue of *Lippincott's Monthly Magazine*. In a chatty, rambling article entitled "Notes of a Base-Ballist," Ward related some of the peculiar problems encountered by the average professional ballplayer of the time; and in the process, he dropped certain intimations of the struggle to come.

For instance, during his first professional days in Renovo, Pennsylvania (1877), Ward tells us, his compensation for playing ball consisted solely of his board and ten dollars a month. After this, he says:

> I went . . . to Williamsport, Pennsylvania, on a promised increase of pay. I say "promised," for before pay-day came the manager had left town, but had neglected to leave his address. For a time I was particularly unfortunate in this respect. During my first ten weeks of professional play, including service with three clubs, I received only ten dollars.

However, with a surprising lack of rancor, Ward adds, "But I make no claims for arrears of pay. I made a living, and, in my circumstances then, that was a relatively larger salary than I have ever received since."

By 1883, the young athlete had made his way along the professional baseball trail farther to the East, where he was destined to play with the New York nine for the ensuing seven seasons. Ward continues:

> During my stay in the League, I have received several tempting offers from clubs of outside organizations, but I have preferred to let well enough alone. There is one unfortunate fact in this connection. It seems that a man cannot, with any credit to himself, play in the same club beyond a definite time. Three years is in most cases the limit. The local public has seen him at his best, when by a combination of good play and good luck, he has done particularly well. It makes this his standard, and expects it from him forever after. If he does that well he is doing only what he should, and if he does less he is playing poorly. I have in mind a number of first-class players who are not at all appreciated at home simply because they

JOHN MONTGOMERY WARD

have overstayed their time. The present reserve-rule, which allows a club to retain a player as long as it wishes, ought to be modified to meet this case.

While conceding that "more than anything else (it had) placed baseball on the basis of a permanent business investment," Ward nevertheless adds:

In speaking of this reserve-rule, I ought to notice an abuse which has sprung up under it. Clubs sometimes retain men for whom they have no possible use, simply for the purpose of selling them to some other club. In this way the player loses not only the benefits a free contract might give, but also the amount paid for his release. For it is plain to infer that if the club was willing to pay that amount for his release they would have been just as willing to pay it to the player in an increased salary . . . In the old days an able-bodied slave sold for from twelve hundred to twenty-five hundred dollars, while the highest price I have yet heard of as being paid for a ball-player was one thousand dollars.

ALBERT G. SPALDING

Here, then, in Ward's own printed words, were incorporated some of the first publicly uttered grievances of the career baseball player, directed primarily at the professional ball clubs' alleged abuse of the reserve rule. And in view of the fact that Ward was the acknowledged leader of the Brotherhood, his words carried added weight and portent.

As for the comparison he drew between the sale price of professional baseball athletes and that of able-bodied slaves, the ratio was radically altered the following year in favor of the ballplayer's value, when Mike "King" Kelly, the great Chicago slugger who helped bring to Chicago five pennants in seven years, was sold to the Boston Club for the then record sum of $10,000 in cash. (A comparable transfer also took place during the subsequent spring, at which time Boston again paid to Chicago $10,000 for the release of their star pitcher, John Clarkson.)

When Albert Spalding, president of the pennant-winning Chicago Club, decided to accept Boston's unprecedented $10,000 offer for the thirty-year old slugger, Chicago's fans were astonished, yet somewhat proud, for Mike "King" Kelly, their hero, had truly commanded a "king's ransom." Still, it was not long before they were singing, to the tune of "Climbing Up The Golden Stairs," the following lyrics:

Arab Kelly's gone and left us,
   Of his presence he's bereft us—
Kelly of the diamond bold.
   He's deserted us for Boston,
Although Albert laid the cost on,
   Ten thousand clear in Puritanic gold.
We surely have the pity
   Of every sister city,
In our loss of Kell, the tricky and the bold.
   But we've entered for the pennant,
And we'll win—depend upon it,
   Notwithstanding Mike has left us in the cold.

Unfortunately, this melodious expression of both self-pity and self-confidence proved to be a form of "singing in the dark," for it was not until the year 1906 that the Chicago Nationals again captured a pennant.

As for "King" Kelly in New England, in 1887 he pounded the ball to the tune of .394; in 1888 he dropped to .318; and in 1889 he was down to .293. The "King" was still an outstanding ballplayer, but as Adrian Anson, his former captain maintained, the man was his own worst enemy. Commenting on Kelly in Boston, Anson, in 1900, said:

He played good ball for a time, but his bad habits soon caused his downfall . . . for baseball and booze will not mix any better than will oil and water. The last time that I ever saw him was at an Eastern hotel barroom, and during the brief space of time that we conversed together he threw in enough whiskey to put an ordinary man under the table . . . He died some years ago [in 1894] in New Jersey, a victim to fast living, and a warning to all ball players.

As stated, John Clarkson, Kelly's teammate, was the second player to be sold for $10,000. Clarkson, according to Anson, was "a really great pitcher, in fact, the best that Chicago ever had." In addition to his clever change of pace and a remarkable curveball, Clarkson had an unorthodox trick that he often employed to advantage: As part of his uniform, he would wear a broad belt with a large polished buckle that would reflect the sun's rays into the opposing batters' eyes. Before the opposition would "catch on" and protest, Clarkson would have put out a number of unsuspecting players.

When Nicholas E. Young, president of the National League, transmitted, on April 5, 1888, the Boston Club's money for the pitcher, Young sent along the following note:

> Dear Spalding: Inclosed herewith I hand you Clarkson's draft for $10,000. Please acknowledge receipt by wire. My commissions on all these $10,000 deals are one box of choice Havanas. My mouth is already watering in anticipation of a first-class smoke. Don't remember of having smoked an imported cigar since the Kelly deal. Too long between smokes. Hope the next one will come sooner. Yours truly, N. E. Young.

These two transactions (Kelly and Clarkson)—cordial as they may have been, judging from Young's note to Spalding—as well as numerous lesser but nonetheless impressive player-money deals between various other clubs, had the effect of bringing the players' grievances into sharper focus when the League formally adopted a standard salary classification code for players in 1888.

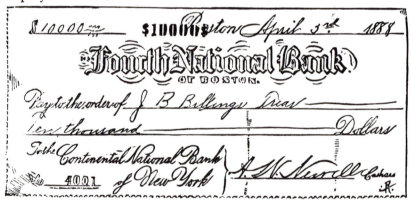

"Fac-Simile of Draft for $10,000
The price paid by the Bostons for the release of John G. Clarkson of the Chicagos."

Hitherto, under the terms of the National Agreement, professional athletes had been paid a maximum salary of $2,000. Nevertheless, in practice, this limit often was exceeded by supplementary private agreements, entered into between players and clubs, through which many players received considerably higher sums of money.

With the adoption of the classification code, however, players henceforth were to be divided into five fixed salary categories, which automatically would restrict their income as follows: A $2,500; B $2,250; C $2,000; D $1,750; E $1,500.

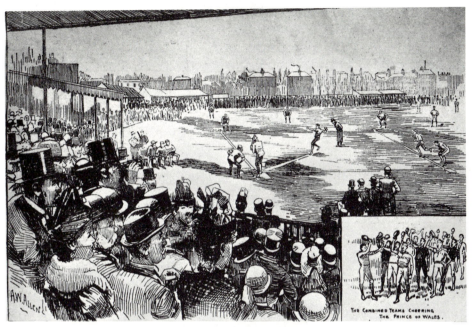

THE AMERICAN BASE-BALL PLAYER AT KENNINGTON OVAL.
From *Pictorial News*, March 23, 1889.

In 1887, the League officially had recognized the National Brotherhood of Baseball Players. In addition, it had accepted a standard player contract, prepared by Brotherhood attorneys. But now, in the year of the great March blizzard that buried the eastern United States under twenty-one inches of snow, the League suddenly decided to restrict and standardize all future player-salary commitments. And the resultant baseball storm, which broke in 1889 over this issue, in its own way rivaled the natural storm of the year before.

It is quite possible that the entire course of events might have taken a different turn had it not been for still another momentous happening that took place during the latter part of 1888 and the early months of 1889—the "Around-the-World Tour" of the Chicago and All-America baseball teams.

This historic undertaking was the inspiration of Albert G. Spalding, who also was involved in the earlier transatlantic tour to England during the previous decade, and Leigh S. Lynch, a prominent theater manager.

Geographically, the globe-girdling trip took the teams westward across

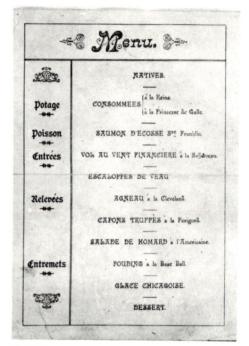

Anglo-French Club Menu.

"A PENNY FOR YOUR THOUGHTS."

(By a Prejudiced Spectator at Kennington Oval on the occasion of the Visit of the American Baseball Team, Monday, March 11, 1889.)

HUMPH! "*New York Herald*" wants to know what we think of the game, and sends round cards of inquiry to take our votes, eh? Hardly formed an opinion yet,—except that it's a beastly day. Wonder how "All America" and "Chicago" like playing their great national game in a fog on a mud-swamp. (*No, my man, I'll not fill up the card yet. Give me time.*) What a lot of left-handers! Fine-built fellows though, and natty dress. Look at that broad-shouldered chap in spotless—*Bang!* By Jove *what* a downer! He's not spotless now either; plastered with Surrey slime from neck to ankle. Doesn't seem to half like it. What *are* they up to? Look to me like a lot of tipsy fellows in a fog. Somebody sprawling every half minute. Find it difficult to follow the game, and as to *the* scoring—well, do they score at all? Br-r-r! it is cold! *All out?* Why, I hardly knew they were in. Score? *Nothing?* And after all that scampering and stumbling! Rum game this!

Ah! *that*'s a good spank! First fair hit I've seen. But what a skyer! Caught? Why, of course; dropped into field's hand as easily as an egg into a cup. What are they doing now? Ah! there's a swipe! *Run, Sir, run!!!* Why, he never stirs? Foul hit? Oh! hang it all! What with misses, and fouls, and skyers, and stumbles, and other mysterious movements I can't understand, *they don't seem to score at all! but we* "don't get no forrader." Yes, they *do* catch well, certainly, and throw straight, only nothing seems to come of it.

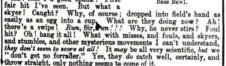

Base Bawl.

Pitcher throws as if he were pelting frogs in a pool. As to Catcher, he looks a cross between *Falstaff*, a fencer, and a Thames diver. Game resembles a glorified—and more dangerous—Rounders, only nobody has made a "rounder" yet, as far as I can see. Gr-r-r! it's cold, yes, and "slow," distinctly slow! Without the prolonged charm of cricket, or the swift, short excitement of foot-ball, but with all the tedium of the one, and all the mud-tumbling of the other. Will that do for our *N. Y. H.* friend? Hardly, I fear.

What, all over? Why, they've done nothing yet. Oh! interval of ten minutes, eh? To take breath, and talk to the PRINCE, I suppose. Hope H.R.H. enjoys it *inside* the Pavilion. *I* don't *outside.* "*Perfect frost?*" "*Utter fraud?*" "*Game for kids?*" "*Boshiest business I ever saw?*" Well, well, Gentlemen, I won't say I don't agree with you, to a certain extent; but *don't* put these sentiments down on the *N. Y. H.* cards. It might lead to—well, a breach of International Amity, eh?

Out again? Well, let's hope they'll make it a little more lively this time. Don't look as spick-and-span as they did at first. Too much Oval mud about them. Why are they *always* tumbling over those indiarubber hot-water cushions—(oh! *bases* are they?)—and dirtying themselves so dreadfully? Part of the game? Humph! Probable, but hardly explanatory. Hooray! First genuine cheer of the afternoon. Good hit, that; what, at Cricket, we should call a "swipe to the boundary," for—how many, four or six is it? Eh! *What?* Game altogether only five to two? Oh! dash it all, that's *too* draggy. Worse than SCOTTON at the wickets.

Humph! Slow again. And, by Jove, *half the Spectators have "mizzled,"* like the rain. Think I shall do likewise, for I'm cold as ice, can't see anything but muddle and mist, and *don't feel to care much for seeing anything more.* Eh? Game's at an end? Well, well—and who's won? Don't know? Neither do I—nor care. Smart fellows, quick as cats, and straight as catapults. Should think they'd make splendid "fields," rattling "throws in," and superb "catches"—at Cricket. But their skill all seems chucked away at this game. "*More scientific than Cricket?*" Bosh! "*Likely to be popular in this country?*" Walker! Fancy a grown-up Rounders, with few hits and scarcely any score, superseding Willow and Stamps! *Don't understand the game?* Well, no, I daresay not, and up to now, somehow, I don't seem to want to.

British reaction to visiting American baseball teams, 1889.

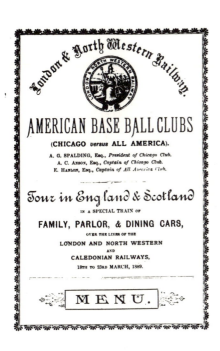

London & North Western
Railway Menu.

AN AMERICAN GIANT ABROAD.

Cartoon depicts the Prince of Wales,
the Lord Mayor of London
and American baseball

the United States from Chicago, across the Pacific to Hawaii, down to New Zealand and Australia, onward to Ceylon and Egypt, through the mainland of Europe, over to England, Scotland, and Ireland, and then home again to the United States. Over 50 games were played during the course of the journey, and the contests served to introduce or better acquaint the peoples of many different lands with the American national pastime.

The traveling ballplayers returned to the United States on Saturday, April 6, 1889. Two days later they played an exhibition game in Brooklyn, and that night the players were officially welcomed home at a festive banquet given in their honor at Delmonico's, one of the most elegant establishments of its kind in New York.

Attending the banquet was a host of notables, not the least of whom was Mark Twain. When the renowned author was introduced by A. G.

OUR BASEBALLISTS IN CAIRO.
February 9, 1889

Mills, the former president of the National League, Twain delivered a brief but hilarious address. This is what he said:

> Though not a native, as intimated by the chairman, I have visited the Sandwich Islands [now called Hawaii]—that peaceful land, that beautiful land, that far-off home of profound repose, and soft indolence, and dreamy solitude, where life is one long, slumberless Sabbath, the climate one long, delicious summer day, and the good that die experience no change, for they but fall asleep in one heaven and wake up in another. And these boys have played baseball there!—baseball, which is the very symbol, the outward and visible expression of the drive and push and rush and struggle of the raging, tearing, booming nineteenth century! One cannot realize it; the place and the fact are so incongruous; it's like interrupting a funeral with a circus. Why, there's no legitimate point of contact, no possible kinship between baseball and the Sandwich Islands; baseball is all fact, the Islands all sentiment. In baseball you've got to do everything just right, or you don't get there; in the Islands you've got to do every-

British reactions to visiting American baseball teams, 1889.

thing just wrong, or you can't stay there. You do it wrong to get it
right, for if you do it right you get it wrong; there isn't any way to
get it right but to do it wrong, and the wronger you do it the righter
it is.

The natives illustrate this every day. They never mount a horse
from the larboard side, they always mount him from the starboard;
on the other hand, they never milk a cow on the starboard side,
they always milk her on the larboard; it's why you see so many short
people there—they've got their heads kicked off . . . As to dress,
the women all wear a single garment, but the men don't. No, the
men don't wear anything at all, they hate display; when they wear
a smile they think they are overdressed . . . And these world wan-
derers who sit before us here have lately looked upon these
things! . . . I envy them that!

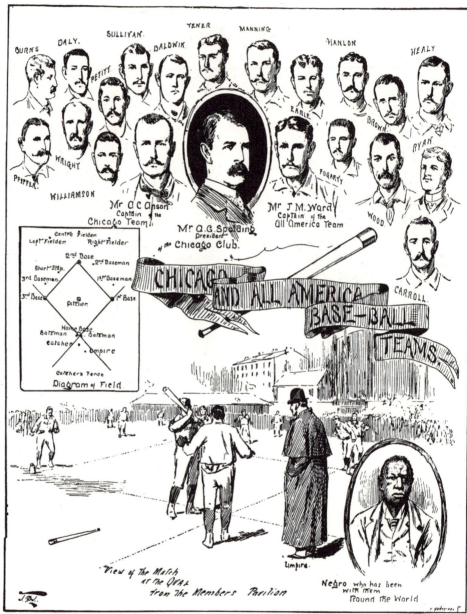

OUR WELCOME GUESTS: AMERICA'S CHAMPION BASEBALL PLAYERS.
Apropos Clarence Duval, the "Negro who has been with them round the world,"
Captain Adrian C. Anson, of the Chicago team, later wrote: "Outside of his
dancing and his power of mimicry he was, however, a 'no account nigger,' and
more than once did I wish that he had been left behind."

LIFE IN LONDON.

"LORD, keep my memory green!"
It was the gentleman in Charles Dickens' "Haunted Man" who gave vent to that pious ejaculation.

But when I visited the Oval on Tuesday last to see the big baseball boom,
I thought it was a prayer that a good many persons present—especially those connected with sporting papers—would do well to include in their diurnal orisons.

THE CATCHER & THE STRIKER

To hear the people talking you would have imagined that Jonathan's national game had never been seen in England before.

Why, I remember as well as if it were but yesterday watching the game played, in the August of 1874, at the Oval, at Prince's, at Lord's, and at the Crystal Palace.

The teams were selected from what were then the two crack clubs of America, the Boston Red Stockings and the Philadelphia Athletic.

And in order to show us how infinitely superior baseball was to cricket, they played our men at their own game and *beat them!*

Yes, it is a fact that those baseballers beat M.C.C., Prince's Club and Ground, Surrey Club and Ground, and two or three provincial clubs at cricket.

They did not play level, of course. They were always allowed odds of eighteen or twenty-two.

But when I say that in the M.C.C. Twelve, there were such men as

A. Lubbock, J. Round, A. C. Lucas, G. Bird, V. E. Walker, E. Lubbock, W. M. Rose, and A. Appleby,

It must be admitted that the Yanks could play a *little* bit at any rate.

This was the strongest team they met, and perhaps had a second innings been played they might have been soundly trounced.

But, as it was, they won by two runs on the first innings.

Their visit, however, was not a success.

The Americans did not arrive in England till the first week in August.

And they were bitterly disappointed at the cold reception they met with.

They expected a national welcome.

Whether their ideas extended so far as to picture the Mayor and Corporation of Liverpool coming down to meet them at the landing-stage, attended by an escort of dragoons,

Is more than I can say.

But they did undoubtedly consider themselves snubbed.

And when they got home they let us have it in style.

They said we were so angry with them for beating us at our own game, that we could not treat them with even bare civility.

They magnified their victories over a few weak scratch elevens into decisive triumphs over the cream of English cricketers.

A BASE BY THE SKIN OF HIS TEETH.

And made such nasty remarks about our insufferable conceit, that I fancy most of us hoped that we had seen the last of American baseball.

He would have been considered a mad prophet indeed who should have ventured to predict that within fifteen years we should see another invasion of baseballers, and that it would be as big a success as the other was a failure.

The reason, however, is not far to seek.

In Mr. A. G. Spalding, our present visitors have got a first-rate showman, which the other lot had not.

He has worked up the excitement beautifully.

Our appetites have been whetted by judiciously-timed paragraphs announcing the enthusiastic receptions which have been accorded to these peripatetic apostles of American sport in all parts of the globe.

And the climax was reached when the announcement burst like a thunderclap upon us, that His Royal Nibs himself would honour the Oval with his presence on the occasion of the first game in London.

It was lucky for Messrs. Spalding and Co. that those floods happened so conveniently.

The show would never had such a good send off from Bristol as it got from the metropolis.

With one consent it appeared to be a settled thing between our visitors and ourselves, that the visit of the baseball team in 1874, should be ignored.

And that the public should, if possible, be induced to believe that Jonathan's national game had never before been witnessed in this country.

Mr. Spalding calculated rightly that few memories nowadays extend over three lustres.

We live too fast and cram too much into our daily lives to be able to treasure events long in our recollection.

And, to tell the truth, the affair of 1874 was hardly worth remembering, except to contrast it with that of 1889.

That contrast I have made entirely to my own satisfaction.

I have seen the baseballers of both periods, and the impression left upon me by the first has not been altered by witnessing the exploits of the second.

CAPTAIN ANSON OF THE CHICAGO'S

But let me get to the Oval at once, and narrate what I saw there.

A less inviting day on which to witness a sport which is essentially a summer one could not well be conceived.

It was cold, wet, misty.

Mr. Mantalini would, no doubt, have described it as "dem'd, demp, moist, unpleasant" weather.

Yet there was a large gathering, and the scene from Kennington Park to the Oval was as bustling and animated as if a big cricket match were on.

How much of this enthusiasm, I asked myself, is due to genuine interest in the new game which we are called upon to admire,

And how much to the knowledge that our Future King is to be among the spectators?

I shall not attempt to answer the question.

I leave every intelligent reader who knows what British snobbery is to answer it for himself.

The first thing that attracted my attention was a net stretched from one end of the pavilion to the other.

I presume this was intended to keep stray balls from crashing in among the spectators.

But its principal effect was to obscure our view of the players, which was quite unnecessary, for the fog answered that purpose much better.

When these much advertised Transatlantic athletes at last stepped out on the green sward,

Their appearance was certainly prepossessing.

They are all men of fine physique, and their uniforms are decidedly becoming.

Chicago are arrayed in grey, with black facings, black caps and stockings.

All America in white, with blue facings and stockings of the same cerulean hue.

On a bright, sunny afternoon their costumes would have looked exceedingly picturesque.

Do not expect me to enter into a description of the niceties of the game.

If I attempted to do so I should plunge you and myself into a fog far thicker than that which spoiled the effect of Tuesday's play.

I note that it is considered the correct thing to describe baseball contemptuously as a sort of glorified rounders.

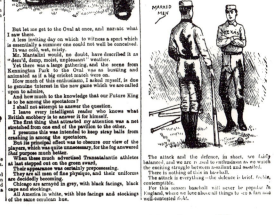

JOHN HEALY   THE AMERICAN PITCHER

This is not fair to the game and its exponents.
Baseball bears as much resemblance to rounders as the primitive cricket of village school-boys to a match between Gentlemen and Players at Lord's or the Oval.

Comparing its present exponents with those of 1874, I do not think that the former are a whit superior to the latter in catching, throwing, and fielding.

These were the great features of interest in the game as it was played here fifteen years ago.

And it was admitted then as now, that the skill and accuracy and activity exhibited were superb.

We were not in those days, it is true, accustomed to such brilliant fielding at cricket as we now see in great matches, thanks to the lessons learned from our Australian cousins.

But in these, which are the most attractive features of baseball, the men of 1874, as far as my memory serves me, were quite equal to those of '89.

And it is certain that the striker was not so terribly handicapped then as he is now.

The game, consequently, as played fifteen years ago, was far more lively and interesting to Englishmen than it is in its present perfection.

The pitcher seems to have it all his own way now.

He has developed marvellously since 1874, both in pace and power over the ball.

The catcher, so far as I remember, wore no mask in 1874.

The lightning expresses of to-day were unknown.

The pitcher's style was more that of old William Clarke, with his slows.

Now he sends them in like bullets from a Martini-Henry, And there is an extraordinary amount of "work" on the ball.

The result is that the unfortunate batsman, be he never so skilful, makes but a tame and feeble display.

His hitting, when he does hit—and he seems to miss oftener than he hits—is wild and erratic.

In fact, he plays quite a secondary part in the game.

The odds against him are so great that our English love of fair play is offended.

We are accustomed to see the batsman take the most prominent position, and all the skill of bowlers and fielders is taxed to the utmost to overcome his stubborn resistance.

MARKED MEN

The attack and the defence, in short, are fairly balanced, and we are roused to enthusiasm as we watch the exciting struggle between assailant and assailed.

There is nothing of this in baseball.

The attack is everything—the defence is brief, feeble, contemptible.

For this reason baseball will never be popular in England, where we love above all things to see a fair and well-contested fight.

The girls will smile, the boys will shout,
The children they will all turn out,
When Johnny comes sailing home.

John Montgomery Ward is home again. He
arrived this morning. The steamship Saale, of
the North German Lloyd line, on which he was
a passenger, reached Sandy Hook at 10 o'clock
last night.

She stopped there until the tide served this
morning, when she sailed up to her dock in
Hoboken.

The famous exponent of the art of good baseball playing was the first voyager to go ashore.
He ran down the gang plank as if he were making a home run to win a game on the Polo
Grounds.

JOHN MONTGOMERY WARD.

He is the same old "Johnny." As handsome
and good-natured as ever.

He wore a silk hat, a dark blue Prince Albert
coat and waistcoat, a pair of light checked wide
trousers, patent leather gaiters and light brown
kid gloves.

There was a "gang" of good fellows on the
pier to welcome him home. They fell on his
neck, so to speak. They shook hands with him.
They whirled him round and round, and seemed
as if they would never tire of looking at him
again.

In the party were George Gore, Nick Engel,
George Floyd and a score of reporters.

Many of them had spent the night on the dock
waiting for the Saale.

TIM KEEFE (Timothy J.)
Pitcher, New York, 1885-1891.
Playing for the New York team of the Players'
League in 1890, he won 17 games while losing 8.

Return of John Montgomery Ward
from The Round the World Baseball
Tour of 1888-89.

But, as suggested earlier, the tour was significant in yet another important respect—namely, in that John Montgomery Ward, the leader of the
Brotherhood of Baseball Players, was one of the tour's playing participants.
And it was while he was out of the country, away from local involve-
ments, that the League announced its new player-salary classification code.
Had he been in the States, the reaction of the players undoubtedly would
have been forceful and immediate; and baseball history probably would
have been different.

But as it was, nothing striking occurred until Ward returned; when
he did, he was denied an immediate audience with League representatives

to discuss matters on behalf of the Brotherhood. Affronted by such treatment of their leader and bolstered by the heightened popularity of the pastime with the public, the players determined to withdraw en masse from the League and form their own baseball circuit. This determination was reinforced by the knowledge that several wealthy financiers were prepared to back the Brotherhood with cash.

Accordingly, on October 30, an announcement was made that a host of men from every professional club had "positively signed contracts to play with the new Ball Players' League;" among the players, there were listed the following individuals: *Boston*—Bennett, Brouthers, Quinn, Kelly; *New York*—Ewing, Murphy, Connor, Hatfield; *Philadelphia*—Clements, Schriver, Myers, Mulvey; *Brooklyn*—Ward, Buckley, Somers, Hines; *Chicago*—Comiskey, Farrell, Darling, Dwyer; *Buffalo*—White, Wise, Rowe, Hoy; *Pittsburg*—Galvin, Dunlap, Glasscock, Denny; *Cleveland*—Stricker, Faatz, Gruber, O'Brien; etc.

On November 4, the Brotherhood issued a further statement to the public, setting forth the players' intentions and offering an explanation and justification for their actions. This is what it said:

> There was a time when the league stood for integrity and fair dealing; to-day it stands for dollars and cents. Once it looked to the elevation of the game and an honest exhibition of the sport; to-day its eyes are upon the turnstile. Men have come into the business for no other motive than to exploit it for every dollar in sight. Measures originally intended for the good of the game have been perverted into instruments for wrong. The reserve rule and the provisions of the national agreement gave the managers unlimited power, and they have not hesitated to use this in the most arbitrary and mercenary way.
>
> Players have been bought, sold, and exchanged as though they were sheep instead of American citizens. "Reservation" became with them another name for property right in the player. By a combination among themselves, stronger than the strongest trust, they were able to enforce the most arbitrary measures, and the player had either to submit or get out of the profession in which he had spent years in attaining proficiency. Even the disbandment and retirement of a club did not free the players from the octopus clutch, for they were then peddled around to the highest bidder.

Of course, the Brotherhood charges did not remain unanswered for long. On November 21, the National League of Professional Base Ball Clubs issued a public statement of its own, declaring that it had "no apology to make for its existence or for its untarnished record of fourteen years." Moreover, under the reserve rule, "the game has steadily grown in favor, the salaries of players have more than trebled and a higher degree of skill been attained." As for "releases for pecuniary considerations . . . except in cases of disbanding or retiring clubs, that right has never been transferred without the player's co-operation and consent, usually at his request, and for his own pecuniary emolument . . . In view of these facts . . . the use of such terms as 'bondage,' 'slavery,' 'sold like sheep,' etc., become meaningless and absurd."

For some time after this first open exchange, the Brotherhood and the League traded similar charges and countercharges in the nation's press, much to the growing distaste of the public. But now the die was cast, and in 1890, the athletes of three major professional circuits—Players' League, American Association, and National League—all took to the baseball diamond and found themselves embroiled in a three-way competition for public interest and support. The result was complete and utter chaos. For the conflicting schedules set up by the different leagues, plus the variety of ugly recriminations aired in public, served only to divide, dismay, and finally, to alienate the fans and patrons of the sport.

On June 20, 1890, old Henry Chadwick, writing in *The Spirit of the South,* wryly observed that "by the end of August if one half of the clubs do not succumb to the pressure of a costly falling off in receipts I shall be much surprised . . . The simple fact is, that the interest in the championship games is gone. No one asks now 'Who leads in the pennant race?' . . . all interest in the championship contests has vanished, or nearly all."

About a month later, on July 17, *The New York Times* declared: "The question what has become of the people who used to go to games of baseball is almost as puzzling as the question what song the Sirens sang, or what name Ulysses took when he hid himself among the women. The one thing that can be said of them with absolute certainty is that they no longer go to see baseball played." Sadly, as had happened so often in the past, the handwriting was now once again upon the wall.

Assessing the situation with the clear and paternal vision that had made him the dean of baseball journalists, "Father" Chadwick wrote:

> The baseball war . . . is not a war of labor or capital as the Brotherhood leaders and their partisan organs would have the baseball world believe. Neither is it a war for the emancipation of so-called "base-

ball slaves." On the contrary it is simply a big strike on the part of high salaried star players for the purpose of ultimately becoming baseball capitalists instead of employees at $5000 a season salaries, aided by a syndicate of Wall Street operators who thought they saw a big bonanza in the hands of the National league magnates.

That just about summed it up. With the loss of public patronage and the continued drain of heavy expenses, the Brotherhood—even with its millionaire backers—was unable to survive financially. Consequently, with the end of the 1890 season, the Players' League simply collapsed and disbanded. And the Brotherhood athletes, finding themselves suddenly without a playing circuit, scrambled with one another to be taken back into the favor of the still-solvent National League and American Association.

As history has borne witness, the "war" between the two leagues was a relatively short-lived affair; but so far as the public was concerned, the national pastime had been dealt an almost mortal blow.

In a sort of eulogy, the *Philadelphia Item* printed the following:

Good-bye, Players' League.

You started out with an avowed purpose, which, in theory, was admirable.

You stuck nobly to your work all through the season, surprising your friends and astounding your enemies.

You ended your season with a flourish, in the purchase of the Cincinnati Club, and then in a sensible but somewhat innocent way proceeded to hold consolidation conferences with your avowed enemy.

You were outwitted. In diplomacy, in finesse, in shrewdness, in keen foresight, you were badly overmatched.

You let your enemy into all the secrets of your camp, and learned next to nothing of your opponent's secrets in return.

Your wily enemy succeeded in dividing you into discordant factions. Suspicion and distrust were implanted where before all had been harmony.

And then your whole organization fell apart.

You have been likened to the fly that upon invitation walked into the spider's parlor.

You have been compared to the man who monkeyed with the buzz-saw—with serious results to himself.

And to-day you are a wreck.

Your life has been a stormy one. Because of your existence many a man is poorer by thousands of dollars. And before long all that will be left of you is a memory—a sad and discouraging memory.

One of those unfortunates who found himself "poorer by thousands of dollars" was the millionaire Albert Johnson, who claimed that in backing the Players' League, he had lost $37,000. Johnson had purchased into both the Cincinnati and the Cleveland clubs of the League; consequently, he emerged a loser on a grand scale.

Edward K. Rife, baseball editor of the *Ohio State Journal*, finding the season's events too "touching" for ordinary comment, composed a song to express his feelings on the subject. Entitled "John Is Eating Crow," and sung to the tune of "Throw Him Down McClusky," the lyrics went as follows:

> **Vanished is the golden vision,**
>   **"Busted" is the deep intrigue.**
> **Bowed the head of Albert Johnson:**
>   **Soupward goes the Players' League.**
> **Mercifully draw the curtain,**
>   **Look not in upon the show;**
> **Turn your heads and pass unheeding—**
>   **Johnny Ward is eating crow.**

Mourning for the Players' League apparently was to be brief, but not so brief as to prevent the *Sporting News*, before the year was out, from shedding one final diminutive tear. This, the paper did, in eight little lines:

> **There was a little Leaguelet**
>   **So promising and bright,**
> **That made a great big blufflet**
>   **And quite a show of fight.**
> **It lived one little yearlet,**
>   **Then dropped into the soup,**
> **So please excuse a tearlet;**
>   **It's not our day to whoop.**

TWELVE

—◆—

BIRTH
OF THE
AMERICAN LEAGUE

"As baseball is no longer a sport, but a business, and a rather low business at that, it must be treated like the stove business and the express business whenever it obstructs the sidewalks or interferes with the clear right of way of pedestrians." So began an editorial in *The New York Times* at the start of the 1891 season. And in a capsule, the sentence aptly expressed the low estate to which the professional pastime had fallen as a result of the Players' League-National League controversy of the year before.

In particular, the editorial was directed against the common practice then engaged in by some newspapers of posting baseball results and inning-by-inning scores on bulletin boards erected on the sidewalk in front of the press offices. In prior days, when fans were flocking to the ball parks and interest in the sport was high, the bulletin boards provided a popular and welcome service, but now, as the *Times* expressed it, "the obstruction and inconvenience the public suffers in consequence of their exposure is altogether intolerable." Furthermore, said the *Times*, "Time and trouble will be saved if the nuisance is suppressed at the very beginning of the season of the so-called game of baseball."

It would be comforting to be able to state that the New York news-paper's attitude was merely an isolated point of view. Unfortunately, such was not the case. The view was an accurate reflection of general opinion, and the public posture of disdain was strongly reinforced by the disheartening baseball events of 1891. For in the aftermath of the 1890 struggle, the National League and the American Association took up the cudgels of conflict where the Brotherhood and the League had so recently laid them down. And, curiously, the "war" between the circuits in 1891, in its own way, was also concerned with a dispute over "reserved" players. However, now the disagreement was on a club-to-club, rather than a player-to-club, level. And the difficulties stemmed from the fact that with the demise of the Brotherhood circuit, the National League clubs immediately proceeded to reserve all available ballplayers, leaving the clubs of the American Association short on playing talent.

In an effort to cope with the situation, the American Association withdrew from the National Agreement and revived the old practice of pirating players wherever and whenever possible. This was a successful tactic for a while, but in this instance, the National League was determined not to prolong the "war." Consequently, mustering all its negotiating skill, plus a vast sum of cash, the League bought out, individually and collectively, the baseball clubs of the American Association.

In a sense, it may be said that the National League swallowed up its rival circuit. For beginning with the 1892 season, the two organizations were consolidated into a single twelve-club circuit, composed of the old eight-franchise League—New York, Brooklyn, Philadelphia, Boston, Cincinnati, Chicago, Pittsburg, and Cleveland—plus four former American Association clubs—St. Louis, Louisville, Baltimore, and Washington.

Then, in a desperate attempt to again generate public enthusiasm for professional baseball, the League pitted these twelve clubs against one another on a dual-season basis. This was accomplished through the simple expedient of dividing the scheduled club contests into twin championships —one terminating in mid-July, the other in the latter part of October. And to make each championship period reasonably exciting, the total number of games played by each club was increased from 140 games to 154, with the overall playing season comparably extended.

But despite the novelty thus injected into the sport, the attempt proved to be a dismal failure. *Reach's Official Base Ball Guide* of 1893 recorded it as follows:

The season of 1892 in base ball will go down into history as one of unusual disappointment. The backers of the game in the United States hoped with the new order of things to retrieve some of the losses which they suffered by the wars of 1890 and 1891 . . . But before midsummer came the fact was proven that it would take at least one more season to get the game back to that state of popularity to which it had grown in 1889 . . . The clubs have this year acknowledged their error in both the double championship and the lengthened season by abolishing both. This year there will be one continuous season, beginning late in April and ending about the first of October.

The public simply was not yet ready to forgive and forget the shenanigans of the two previous years. And they demonstrated this feeling by staying away from the professional ball parks.

However, this does not mean that all interest in the pastime was lost. For it must be recalled that the nation as a whole still was in the throes of "athleticism," and a good percentage of the public still was "ball crazy."

Indeed, in 1891, it was even reported that baseball was being used as a form of therapy in the treatment of mental illness—a revolutionary development at the time. Details of the "treatment" were divulged to the general public in a brief two-paragraph release dated *Middletown, N. Y. January 10th,* under a heading that read, "Baseball For The Insane. The Remedial Virtues of the National Game Recognized." And the paragraphs read as follows:

The remedial virtues of the national game of baseball in the treatment of mental disorders are dwelt upon with considerable emphasis by Dr. Selden H. Talcott, the Medical Superintendent of the Middletown State Homeopathic Hospital for the Insane, in his annual report for 1890 to the State Legislature. This institution is the only asylum for the insane in the country which recognizes the game as the best form of outdoor amusement that can be provided for its inmates, and which maintains among its patients a regularly organized and equipped amateur baseball club of acknowledged skill and reputation. The club has been in active existence for two seasons.

In his report for 1890 Dr. Talcott reiterates with emphasis his views of the highly beneficial character of this form of outdoor amusement. He also calls attention to the record of the remarkable achievements of the asylum club during the season lately closed. The asylum team has had skillful training by Captain J. C. Degnan, a noted amateur player, and has also enjoyed the advantages of plenty of time and perfect grounds for practice. The result is seen in a record for the season of twenty-five games played with noted amateur and semi-professional clubs, of which games the asylum nine has won twenty-one and lost only four.

As for the fans at large, Caspar W. Whitney, writing in the September 1893 issue of *The Fortnightly Review,* declared that although "in the last year or so, the better class of American sportsmen appear to have lost all interest in professional baseball," the pastime itself "has, nevertheless, spread all over the country, and now attracts the same spectators, and in equal numbers, that professional ball did in the days when it was decent, clean sport."

Elaborating on this statement, Mr. Whitney continued, "The contests every May and June between the teams of Harvard, Yale, and Princeton attract great crowds, and of the very best people." In addition, "Outside of college baseball . . . there are hundreds upon hundreds of amateur clubs scattered all over the country."

And finally, to personify in individual terms the still popular status of the game, Mr. Whitney concluded, "every small boy owns a bat and a ball."

However, even as Caspar Whitney was citing college baseball as annually attracting "great crowds, and of the very best people," others were equally concerned that the spirit of "athleticism" was slowly infecting university campuses with negative influences and morally harmful values.

That this was so is borne out by a stinging editorial entitled "The Athletic Craze," printed by *The Nation* barely three months after Mr. Whitney's remarks were published. Focusing its critical eye specifically upon football (which sporting season then happened to be in progress), but at the same time "respectfully" directing the attention of college faculties to "all college games," this is what *The Nation* said:

> We are informed on good authority that Yale spent last year about $47,000 on athletics, and the team went to Springfield the other day with three drawing-room cars and fifty men as substitutes, doctors, trainers, rubbers, and cooks. The receipts on Thursday from the gate-money in New York cannot have fallen far short of $50,000. It was earned by exhibiting feats of strength and agility by scholars and gentlemen before an enormous city crowd, in which the gambling fraternity and the prostitutes were very prominent.

THE WHALERS PLAYING BASEBALL ON THE ICE
In an article describing the whalers, Brig.-Gen. Frederick Funston wrote:
"The colored brother, too, was there, a dozen of him,
and several of the players were negroes."

Obviously, Mr. Whitney and *The Nation* had seen two quite different types of audiences at recent college contests. But generally, the fact remained that the more exciting sporting games and events in the land were being staged by amateur school teams, not by the professional athletes.

And exotic as it may seem—and difficult to believe—during the years 1894 and 1895, some of the most exciting baseball of all was being played not on the mainland of the United States, but (of all places!) at one the bleakest spots on earth—on the frozen waters off Herschel Island, five hundred miles inside the Arctic Circle.

During those years, a fleet of steam whaling ships—17 in all—became icebound in the Arctic Ocean, near the mouth of the Mackenzie River. The ships were owned by two New Bedford whaling enterprises, J. R. Wing and William Lewis & Co., and by two San Francisco firms, Roth & Blum Co. and the Pacific Steam Whaling Co.

As fate would have it, aboard one of the ships there happened to be a supply of baseball equipment (bats, balls, etc.) that provided the stimulus for the formation among the 700 whalingmen of the unlikely "Arctic Baseball League," a loose organization of seven separate clubs. During the long winter months (temperatures ranged from 40 to 50 degrees below zero), the clubs worked out plans for a league competition for the Arctic Whalemen's Pennant, a proud piece of twill cloth nailed to the handle of a broom. And when the season of the long night was over, the Arctic baseball season began.

A complete ballfield was measured out on the smooth frozen surface of the ocean; sawdust-filled bags marked the bases; and flags set into the ice delineated the foul lines. Players wore sealskin or deerskin garments, deerskin gloves, and boots. League games were played twice weekly, and scrub games almost daily. Frequently, the Esquimaux, who lived on nearby Herschel Island, were interested spectators, and on several occasions, they even participated in the scrub contests.

The Arctic Baseball League, probably the hardiest and most distinctive of its kind, literally "melted away" after its second season, in 1895, when the ice finally thawed and the whaling fleet steamed away.

The impact of such a loss to the sport, of course, is purely of passing interest. The Arctic Baseball League was simply an oddity and, as such, totally unrelated to events in the United States, where professional baseball was actually fighting for its very survival. For throughout the last decade of the nineteenth century, the clubs, athletes, investors, and all the other individuals who derived their income from professional league games were concerned mainly with the fact that the public at large no longer was interested in watching them.

In an essay written and published in 1894, George Santayana, the American philosopher, made certain astute observations about the role played by spectators at athletic contests. This is what he wrote:

> Athletic sports are not children's games; they are public spectacles in which young men, carefully trained and disciplined, contend with one another in feats of strength, skill, and courage. Spectators are

indispensable, since without them the victory, which should be the only reward, would lose half its power. For as Pindar, who knew, tells us:

"Success
Is half the prize, the other half renown.
Who both achieves, he hath the perfect crown."

But for professional baseball, "half the prize" was not enough; since without spectators—and more importantly, *without the admission fees paid by spectators*—the clubs could not long survive.

Fortunately, by the end of 1895, the public attitude had so changed that *Reach's Official Base Ball Guide* was able to report that "for the first time since base ball became a professional game, every club in the National League ended the year a financial winner." This achievement the *Guide* attributed to two facts: (1) "Not a breath of scandal marred the season;" and (2) "one of the closest, cleanest, most satisfactory campaigns since the National League was organized in 1876."

But if 1895 was an outstanding year for professional baseball, the ensuing half-dozen years or so—which ushered in both a new baseball era and a new century—saw the game's fortunes fluctuate from extremes of high public regard to levels of low repute, then back up again to high esteem.

Various factors contributed to this state of flux, among which were the following: the hard times and depression of 1896; the unsettling influences of the Spanish-American War of 1898; the unsuccessful attempts of various syndicates to revive the old American Association; the relapse of League competition to utterly unmasked rowdyism; and the rise of the American League.

Particularly damaging to the professional pastime during these years, however, was the degeneration of sportsmanship to more and more ruffian-like exhibitions on the ballfield. For it was at the actual contests themselves that the public had the opportunity of weighing and evaluating at first hand the quality of competition and fair play, which combination, in the long run, constitutes the essence of good baseball.

By 1898, this unwholesome development had reached such ugly proportions that *Reach's Official Base Ball Guide* was compelled to take official note of it. Speaking of the previous campaign, the *Guide* said, "the season was notable for many disgraceful brawls upon the field, indicating a steady decline in the decorum of players, and inducing the magnates to adopt strict regulations in order to prevent a recurrence of them in the future."

A long list of incidents was cited, a sampling of which are the following:

> May 23d—O'Brien, of the Washingtons, spat in Lange's face in a game at Chicago, and the two engaged in a fist fight. Both were subsequently fined by President Young at the Chicago club's demand. May 26th—Crowd followed Umpire Hurst to his dressing room after the game and assaulted him without serious injury to the plucky official. June 24th—Monte Cross, of the St. Louis club struck Umpire Sheridan in the game at Pittsburg.

Other incidents were cited for July 8, 16, 31, for August 4, 6, 9, and so on.

The "strict regulations" mentioned by the *Guide* were embodied in a resolution adopted by the National League on March 2, 1898. The preamble called it:

> A measure for the suppression of obscene, indecent and vulgar language upon the ball field by players engaged in playing a game of ball during the championship season, while under contract to a club member of the National League and American Association of professional ball clubs, to the end that the game may retain its high position as respectable and worthy of the confidence and support of the refined and cultured classes of American citizenship.

Section 7 of the resolution stated:

> The penalties for using obscene, indecent or vulgar language within the meaning and intent of this measure are entirely within the discretion of the tribunal, and may be suspension for days, for months, for the unexpired season, for a year, or for life, according to the conditions, circumstances and nature of the offense, it being the sentiment of the League that creates this law, that an unwarranted, unprovoked and brutal use of vulgarity to a spectator or within the presence of spectators and within the hearing of ladies should debar the offender forever from services with his club, or any other club, member of this League, or subject to its jurdisdiction.

However, despite the stringent penalties adopted in March, by September 12, *The New York Times* was saying:

> Professional baseball, as carried on at the present day, is without power to excite popular enthusiasm . . . The attendance has fallen off materially in this city, where squabbles over the rules, the exchange

of approbrious epithets, and fines, and wide and vigorous "kicking" at the umpire's decisions by the players, are salient features of every game.

It is not sufficient to say that "rowdyism" on the ballfield has injured the popularity of the game. That feature has driven ladies and gentlemen away from the ballfield, but it is not the rowdyism as such, that keeps the mob away . . . but the spirit which lies behind it, that has killed professional baseball.

And nearly two years later, by July 25, 1900, the influential newspaper was saying:

There was a time when baseball was the National game of this country. It is so now only in name, and chiefly because it is not played in other lands . . . Even in the colleges, where the game is played in the highest and most sportsmanlike spirit of rivalry, it has taken a comparatively low position in recent years.

The "low position" of college baseball apparently sank to an even lower level the following year when both *The Princeton Alumni Weekly* and *The Yale Alumni Weekly* took the undergraduates of their respective schools to task for excessive cheering at games.

Said the Princeton publication:

The adoption of a noiseless game at this particular time, when so many other colleges are playing noisy baseball, and so many people are talking about it, would do more good to Princeton than winning the championship.

And observed the Yale weekly:

A constant din, which prevents conversation even on the grandstand and which makes it difficult for players to understand each other, and which certainly does affect men who have nerves, is a very questionable part of a university contest. It will be done away with sooner or later, and we would like very much to see Yale lead in the reform of cheering.

But the Yale students, noted for their wit and waggishness, responded in *The Yale News* to the Alumni suggestion with the following amusing sarcasm:

The conduct of the university at Saturday's game was rough and ungentlemanly. Several ladies were unable to say a word during the din. Should such conduct be allowed? No; a far better plan could

A COLLEGIATE GAME, 1889.
The ladies obviously are interested in viewing everything but the game. Note in particular the lady in the foreground with binoculars trained on the grandstand instead of the ballfield.
From *Harper's Weekly*, August 31, 1889.

be adopted. Let the baseball management furnish blanks to all on entering the field, and those desiring to express their enthusiasm may write "Bravo" or "Well played" and hand the blanks to the captain, who will read them to the audience at the end of each inning. By bringing along a number of fast and expert writers the visiting teams would be at no disadvantage and all will be fair and square.

But even as all these things were going on, the stage was being set in professional circles for the event that finally established the national pastime on the foundation upon which it rests today. That event was the birth and growth of the American League, the so-called "junior" circuit of the two major leagues.

Actually, the American League began originally as the Western League, a minor circuit that was organized in 1893. Byron "Ban" Johnson was the guiding spirit and first president of the young organization; it was he who saw it through its difficult formative years, until 1927, when Ernest S. Barnard finally succeeded him as president.

In October 1899, the Western League, with a view toward eastward expansion, officially changed its name to the "American League." It was felt that the new name would embrace a national concept, rather than merely convey a sectional interest. And with the older National League's announced intention of reducing its twelve-club circuit to only eight franchises, "Ban" Johnson saw the possibility of moving his new circuit up to big-league status.

This he proceeded to do by establishing Charles A. Comiskey's St. Paul team in a Chicago franchise, and by placing the former Grand Rapids team in Cleveland. These changes thus brought into being the first American League baseball circuit, composed of the following eight clubs: Chicago, Cleveland, Detroit, Milwaukee, Buffalo, Minneapolis, Kansas City, and Indianapolis.

THE "PREPARATORY POSITION"
FOR PITCHING
From *The Art of Pitching
and Fielding*, 1885-6.

But as the American League sought to entrench itself officially in 1901 as a major baseball circuit by expanding to Philadelphia, Washington, and Baltimore, the senior National League suddenly reacted with fierce and determined opposition. The result was that the new organization withdrew from the National Agreement, and two more years of baseball "war" ensued.

By 1903, however, with both sides grown weary and concerned that the very image of the national pastime had fallen victim to the prolonged conflict, a lasting peace was finally concluded.

A new National Agreement was signed, and the young American League—now with franchises in New York, Boston, Philadelphia, Cleveland, Chicago, Washington, Detroit, and St. Louis—was accepted as a baseball organization of equal status by its rival, the old National League.

A National Commission, composed of the presidents of the two circuits and a selected chairman, also was established to govern the organized sport as a supreme three-man authority. The Honorable August Herrmann was chosen first chairman, while Byron Johnson of the American League and Harry C. Pulliam of the National League were the other two members.

Thus, through the crucible of turbulence, tribulation, and years of conflict, the basic major-league structure of the American national pastime was forged and formed.

THIRTEEN

◆

THE DAWN
OF
MODERN BASEBALL

The year 1903, which marked baseball's new National Agreement, was noteworthy in yet another respect: It was the year Henry Ford organized the Ford Motor Company.

As increasing numbers of primitive automobiles made their appearance on the nation's roads, the raucous cry "Get a horse!" began to be heard throughout the land. By the end of 1910, however, almost half a million motor vehicles were registered in the United States, and the days of the horse as a common sight seemed to be numbered.

It was precisely this situation that inspired Hubert R. Kotterman to compose the following:

> Some people think, absurdly, too,
>   That the horse's day is o'er;
> Fact is, the time is nearly due
>   When we'll need him more and more.
>
> Two big leagues now are in the field,
>   And others are expected;
> To any thinker 'tis revealed
>   The horse can't be neglected.

We have ceased to be horse lovers,
As the term was once applied,
But to make our baseball covers
We've got to have his hide!

And indeed this was so. The fears that had initially plagued the National League that competition from another circuit would be financially disastrous proved to be entirely without foundation. For instead of dividing the interest and loyalties of the fans, the rivalry and competition that was generated between the two leagues served only to heighten interest and bring more and more patrons out to the ball games.

At the start of the century, for example, the combined attendance at games of the two warring leagues was slightly over 3,600,000 persons. By 1905, the figure had risen to over 5,800,000. And by the end of the first decade, it was reported that over 7,250,000 persons had paid to see major league contests during the 1910 baseball season.

Various factors contributed to the steady and impressive rise in popularity of the sport, not the least of which was the fact that exciting baseball was being played in both leagues.

In the senior National circuit, Fred C. Clarke's Pittsburgh nine, sparked by the heavy slugging of its crack shortstop, John P. "Honus" Wagner, captured the first three championships of the twentieth century in a row. Wagner had garnered the league batting crown for the first time in 1900; then, starting with the season of 1903, he went on to lead the league in batting for the next seven out of nine years, helping to bring Pittsburgh its fourth pennant in 1909.

In the great Eastern metropolis, John J. McGraw, the colorful manager of the New York Giants, was embarking on a memorable career that was to span three decades. In that overall period, McGraw led the Giants to a total of ten National League pennants and three World Series championships.

During the first decade and a half of McGraw's leadership, the fabulous Christy "Big Six" Mathewson was the Giants' pitching ace. Mathewson's wizardry on the mound not only contributed in large measure to his team's success but it also made his name legendary in baseball annals.

Mathewson, who has been rated as one of the all-time great pitchers of baseball, won over 370 games during the course of his National League career. In twelve consecutive years, he won twenty games or more per season; and over a seventeen-year period, he averaged twenty-three victories annually.

But it was in 1905 that "Big Six" scored his most memorable triumph —he thrice shut out Connie Mack's Philadelphia Athletics in as many World Series encounters; and in the process, he allowed the Mack-men a meager three-game total of only fourteen hits.

Joe McGinnity, Mathewson's pitching colleague, accounted for the remaining Giant victory—also a shutout performance—and the four victories gave New York the championship.

Oddly enough, the single Series game lost to Philadelphia during that postseason classic fell into the same shutout pattern of the other games played. For the Athletics, behind the 4-hit hurling of Charlie "Chief" Bender, defeated the Giants and McGinnity in the second contest of the five by a score of 3 to 0.

Incidentally, the World Series of 1905 was notable in yet another respect. It marked the start of the so-called modern era of World Series competition.* And, coincidentally, McGraw and his Giants, besides winning the Series flag that year, also figured prominently in the controversial circumstances surrounding the event's inauguration. Briefly, this is the story:

At the close of hostilities between the new American League and the old National League in 1903, a postseason world championship competition was arranged between the respective pennant-winning teams of both circuits: the Pittsburgh Nationals and the Boston Americans. The affair, however, was a more or less private contest since the newly created National Commission took no part in the arrangements.

In 1904, Boston again captured the American League pennant, and following the precedent of the previous year, the club immediately invited McGraw's Giants, the National League winners, to a postseason Series duel. But this time, the New England team met with an unexpected rebuff; for McGraw, still nursing a personal animosity toward American League President Byron Johnson over the recent baseball conflict, declined the Boston invitation to play. The result was that no World Series was held that year.

* Postseason competition to determine a "world champion" baseball team actually dates all the way back to the year 1882, when the pennant-winning Cincinnati club of the American Association and the Chicago champions of the National League played a curtailed, unsanctioned "Series" that ended in a tie, each team winning one of the two games played. Then, from 1884 through 1890, seven other sanctioned "Series" were staged between the champion teams of the two circuits. The "Temple Cup Series" was another such competition that was held annually from 1894 through 1897, but this Series was exclusively an intra-National League event between the pennant winner and the second-place club.

It is possible that the World Series as we know it may never have become an annual institution had it not been for McGraw's petulant action in 1904. For the public clamor that arose as a consequence forced the issue of postseason games into the open; and it was McGraw's employer himself, John T. Brush, owner of the New York club, who proposed the formal World Series code of rules that ultimately was accepted by the two leagues and the National Commission. That code governed the World Series of 1905, and it largely governs the classic today.

But remarkable as the New York and Pittsburgh Nationals were during the first five years of the century, during the following five years, both of these clubs played in the shadow of Frank Chance's great Chicago nine. From 1906 through 1910, Chance's men won the pennant four out of five times, and twice—in 1907 and 1908—they captured the World Series championship.

It was during this five-year period that Mordecai "Three-Finger" Brown came into prominence, averaging better than twenty-five games won per season for the Cubs, despite the fact that two fingers from his right pitching hand were missing.

In addition, the phrase "Tinker to Evers to Chance" acquired legendary renown as the precision double-play combination of the Chicago infield made almost day-to-day history on the diamond.

Contributing further interest to the decade was the famous Fred Merkle blunder, which subsequently cost New York the 1908 National League pennant. The youthful Giant player, in the final moments of a game with Chicago, neglected to touch second base and was declared out on a play that prevented his team from scoring the winning run. The contest consequently ended in a tie; and when the two league-leading clubs wound up the season also in a tie, the Chicagoans won the replay game and the pennant.

However, all the excitement was not confined to the National League. In the American circuit, two names were becoming baseball bywords— Napoleon "Nap" Lajoie and Tyrus "Ty" Cobb.

Lajoie, first with Philadelphia and then with Cleveland, practically dominated American League batting in the early seasons of the century, clouting at an average of over .400 in the century's very first year.

Cobb, on the other hand, coming along a little later, established for himself one of the great reputations—if not the greatest—in baseball history. A commemorative tablet, lodged in the Baseball Hall of Fame at

TY COBB.

Cooperstown, New York, pays him the following tribute: "Tyrus Raymond Cobb. Detroit-Philadelphia, A. L.—1905–1928. Led American League in batting twelve times and created or equalled more major league records than any other player. Retired with 4,191 major league hits."

Almost all of Cobb's records can best be described by the single superlative word "most," such as: *most* times at bat, hits made, runs scored; *most* years batting .300 or over; *most* singles, triples, games in a major league; etc.

From 1907 straight through 1919, Cobb held the annual batting crown of the American League, a record interrupted only in 1916 by "Tris" Speaker, of Cleveland, who beat Cobb's impressive .371 average for that year by registering a .386 average of his own.

It is of interest to note that in the year Ty Cobb won his initial batting laurels, 1907, the seeds of the Doubleday-Cooperstown legend concerning the origin of baseball also were sown. In a capsule, this is how it happened:

For many years—dating back even to the latter part of the nineteenth century—a friendly squabble on the subject had been simmering between A. G. Spalding, the sporting-goods magnate and early baseball star, and Henry Chadwick, the so-called "Father of Baseball." Chadwick had always maintained that baseball was simply a sophisticated version of the old English children's game of rounders. Spalding had contended that baseball was far removed from the early English game and that the American national pastime had exclusive roots in this country.

At last, in 1907, a distinguished committee was formed, at Spalding's suggestion and with Chadwick's approval, to investigate and settle the issue once and for all. The committee was composed of the following seven gentlemen: former president of the National League A. G. Mills, chairman, and Morgan G. Bulkeley, Nicholas E. Young, Albert Reach, George Wright, Arthur P. Gorman, and James E. Sullivan.

Although each had at one time been connected with baseball and sports in some important way or other, none of the committeemen really took their investigative assignment seriously, for all regarded the matter as a more or less amiable disagreement between two elderly gentlemen, Spalding and Chadwick. This being the committee's attitude, little or nothing was done in the nature of earnest research until finally, shortly before 1908, Chairman Mills, in the name of the committee, came up with a "report" that he alone had drafted.

The Mills report, without offering in evidence anything more substantial than a number of vague, circumstantial, and speculative opinions and statements, attributed the invention of the game of baseball to Abner Doubleday, who ostensibly played it first at Cooperstown, New York, in the year 1839.

How Mills arrived at these conclusions is unknown, but it has been suggested that his report was simply a sentimental personal testimonial of his own fabrication to the memory of a dear and very old friend, Abner

ABRAHAM G. MILLS
Third President of National League and author of the Mills report (1907), which attributed the invention of the game of baseball to Abner Doubleday, 1839, at Cooperstown, New York. From an old portrait
Root & Tinker, Tribune Building, New York 1884.

Doubleday. And if the facts were either incorrect or distorted, Mills is purported to have thought, the difference could be of little consequence so many years afterward.

However, three decades later, the difference proved to be very consequential indeed. For it was precisely upon the findings of the Mills document that baseball's Hall of Fame and National Museum were founded, and on which the centennial celebration of baseball's alleged birth was based.

So much advance publicity was given to the proposed celebration that to commemorate the occasion, the Post Office of the United States even went so far as to issue a special 3¢ baseball stamp, first placed on sale at Cooperstown on June 12, 1939, exactly one hundred years after the game was alleged to have been invented.*

 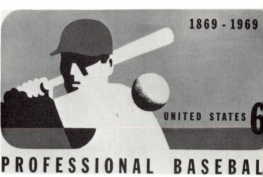

U.S. commemorative baseball stamps, 1939 and 1969.

All of these things were sponsored by or promoted through the offices of the then commissioner of baseball, Kenesaw M. Landis, and a large segment of the sporting press, whose motives were to generate more interest in the national pastime during the great depression years of the thirties.

Thus it was that the curious and entirely imaginary Doubleday legend was born and fostered.

Oddly, the year 1907 was significant in still another respect. It was the year in which an obscure little book was published under the title *Sol. White's Official Base Ball Guide;* and the book contained what the author called a "History of Colored Base Ball."

In light of the genuine breakthrough made by black athletes into the ranks of major-league professional baseball since the end of World War II, the account makes most informative and interesting reading today. For besides dealing with many facets of professional black ball teams of the late nineteenth and early twentieth centuries—such as the Philadelphia Orions, New York Gorhams, Cuban Giants, and Page Fence Giants—Mr. White, a former all-around player on many black nines and organizer of the Philadelphia Giant ball club, candidly discusses some of the problems faced by blacks for so long a time in connection with the American national pastime.

---

* On September 24, 1969, the Post Office issued another commemorative stamp —this time a 6¢ stamp—to celebrate the one-hundredth anniversary of professional baseball.

This is what Sol. White said in 1907:

In no other profession has the color line been drawn more rigidly than in base ball. As far back as 1872 the first colored ball player of note playing on a white team was Bud Fowler, the celebrated promoter of colored ball clubs, and the sage of base ball. Bud played on a New Castle, Pa., team that year. Later, the Walker brothers, Fleet and Weldy, played on prominent college teams of the West. Fleet Walker has the distinction of being the only known colored player that ever played in one of the big leagues. In 1882 Walker caught for Toledo in the old American Association. At this time the Walker brothers and Bud Fowler were the only negroes in the profession.

In 1886 Frank Grant joined Buffalo, of the International League.

In 1887 no less than twenty colored ball players were scattered among the different smaller leagues of the country.

Derogatory illustration in *Harper's Weekly*,
the self-styled "Journal of Civilization," 1878.

With Walker, Grant, Stovy, Fowler, Higgins and Renfro in the International League, White, W. Walker, N. Higgins and R. Johnson in the Ohio League, and others in the West, made 1887 a banner year for colored talent in the white leagues. But this year marked the beginning of the elimination of colored players from white clubs. All the leagues, during the Winter of 1887 and 1888, drew the color line, or had a clause inserted in their constitutions limiting the number of colored players to be employed by each club.

This color line had been agitated by A. C. Anson, Captain of the Chicago National League team for years. As far back as 1882, Anson, with his team, landed in Toledo, O., to play an exhibition game with the American Association team. Walker, the colored catcher, was a member of the Toledos at the time. Anson at first absolutely refused to play his nine against Walker, the colored man, until he was told he could either play with Walker on the team or take his nine off the field. Anson in 1887 again refused to play the Newark Eastern League club with Stovy, the colored pitcher, in the box. Were it not for this same man Anson, there would have been a colored player in the National League in 1887. John M. Ward, of the New York club, was anxious to secure Geo. Stovy and arrangements were about completed for his transfer from the Newark club, when a howl was heard from Chicago to New York . . . Just why Adrian C. Anson, manager and captain of the Chicago National League Club, was so strongly opposed to colored players on white teams cannot be explained. His repugnant feeling, shown at every opportunity, toward colored ball players, was a source of comment throughout every league in the country, and his opposition, with his great popularity and power in base ball circles, hastened the exclusion of the black man from the white leagues.

The colored players are not only barred from playing on white clubs, but at times games are cancelled for no other reason than objections being raised by a Southern ball player, who refuses to play against a colored ball club. These men from the South who object to playing are, as a rule, fine ball players, and rather than lose their services, the managers will not book a colored team.

The colored ball player suffers great inconvenience, at times, while travelling. All hotels are generally filled from the cellar to the garret when they strike a town. It is a common occurrence for them to arrive in a city late at night and walk around for several hours before getting a place to lodge.

Calling attention to another area in which the professional black player was suffering gross injustice, Mr. White cited the disparity in salaries paid to white players and those paid to blacks in 1906. According to

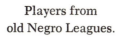

SOL WHITE, Capt., 1st B.
Philadelphia Giants

DAN MCCLELLAN, P.
Philadelphia Giants

JOHN HILL, S.S.
Cuban X-Giants

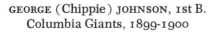

ROBERT JACKSON, C.
Chicago Unions

FRANK GRANT, 2nd B.
Buffalo International
League, 1888

GEORGE (Chippie) JOHNSON, 1st B.
Columbia Giants, 1899-1900

W. W. WALKER, C.
Akron, Ohio League Team, 1887

WILLIAM WHYTE, P.
Original Cuban Giants

the figures presented, the average season's salary drawn by a major league white player was $2,000; that of a minor leaguer, $571. But the average salary drawn by a black professional (who, if not for his color might have been earning $2,000 annually in the major leagues) was a mere $466.

Fortunately, it can be said that such conditions in baseball no longer prevail. The breach came in 1946, when Jack R. Robinson, a young black athlete from UCLA, was given a contract and brought into the Brooklyn Dodger organization by Branch Rickey, president of the club. After spending a year with the club's farm team in Montreal, Robinson joined the Dodgers. The rest is history.

Jackie captured the imagination of the public almost immediately with his brilliant playing and good sportsmanship; and over the years he collected a host of laurels until his retirement in 1956.

It is poetic justice that in the very same Hall of Fame at Cooperstown, where an inscribed plaque honors the feats and memory of Adrian C. Anson, the man most responsible for barring blacks from the big leagues, there now is installed a similar plaque extolling Jackie Robinson, the first black ballplayer in modern times to crack the racial barrier.

Also, in the aftermath of the assassination, in Memphis, Tennessee, of the Reverend Dr. Martin Luther King, Jr., the great civil-rights leader, which occurred during the week preceding the start of the 1968 baseball season, as a gesture of respect to the memory of the black martyr and in mourning for his loss to all mankind, the official opening games were postponed for the first time in the history of the national pastime.

Black ballplayers were often the butt of jokes and cartoons
in the nineteenth century.

It remains only to be added that since Robinson's acceptance on the basis of his skill alone, black and dark-skinned Latin athletes by the score have appeared and played in major-league uniforms all over the country. The public not only has welcomed them but, in many cases, idolized them.

Some of the more familiar names (besides Jackie Robinson) are

Willie Mays, Roy Campanella, Don Newcombe, Hank Aaron, Ernie Banks, Maury Wills, and Roberto Clemente. All of these athletes have one thing in common—aside from the dark color of their skin. Each has won at least one most-valuable-player award; Roy Campanella, the second black player to have been elected to the Hall of Fame, has won three, and both Ernie Banks and Willie Mays have won two.

Willie Mays, who has banged out more home runs than any other major-league ballplayer besides Babe Ruth, has the added distinction of having won the National League batting crown in 1954, and of having led the league in home runs hit in 1955, 1962, 1964, and 1965; while Maury Wills, for his part, now has accumulated more stolen bases than the immortal Ty Cobb, who once held the record at 892.

Other dark-skinned athletes who have made the major leagues include such men as Larry Doby, Joe Black, Sam Jethroe, Luke Easter, Leroy "Satchel" Paige, Elston Howard, Juan Marichal, Al Downing, Jim Gilliam, Hector Lopez, Frank Robinson, Lou Brock, Bob Gibson, Tommy Agee, Cleon Jones, Curt Flood, Rico Cortez, Tony Perez, Dock Ellis, Vida Blue, and many more, all of whom are equally competent athletes. Indeed, in 1968, nearly 30 percent of all players in the National League alone were nonwhite; and in 1968, too, the barrier to blacks on the executive level was bridged when Monte Irvin, the former star outfielder of the New York Giants, was appointed assistant director of promotion and public relations for baseball in the office of the commissioner, William D. Eckert.

Finally, in a belated effort to rectify some of the injustices of the past, the major leagues, in 1971, established a system to honor baseball stars from the old Negro leagues by electing them to the Hall of Fame. Fittingly, the first player so honored was that "ageless" veteran, Satchel Paige, who is said to have pitched, over a 22-year period on all-black teams, as many as 2,500 games, winning most of them. And in 1972, Josh Gibson and Walter "Buck" Leonard, known as the Babe Ruth and Lou Gehrig, respectively, of the Homestead Grays of Pittsburgh, joined the elite at Cooperstown.

Not only have the racial bars been done away with, but the old salary inequities discussed by Sol. White in 1907 also have vanished. In fact, some of the highest-paid players today are blacks; and Willie Mays, for example, is one of the very few men of any race ever to have been paid more than $150,000 for a single season's work.

On a "Willie Mays Night" in New York on May 3, 1963, the President of the United States sent Mays the following telegram:

I would like to join the many loyal fans at the Polo Grounds tonight honoring your achievements in the world of baseball. This honor is well deserved and I know we can look forward to many years of the exciting spectacle of Willie Mays at bat and in the field. My very best wishes to all of your friends tonight.—John F. Kennedy.

However, prejudice and bigotry in American baseball were not confined solely to the black man before the modern era. Consider the following, which was published in a so-called book of humor by "Jack" Regan and Will E. Stahl, in the year 1910: "In looking over the list of names comprising the American and National Leagues we fail to discover any of those well worn Semitic cognomens, such as Moses, Abraham, Ikey, Solomon, Aaron, etc., or the tribe of numerous 'Skys.' Something wrong. Is the work too arduous?"

Unfortunately, something *was* wrong, but mainly with the writers Regan and Stahl, and with men like them. For the fact is that anti-Semitism did for many years fester in the national pastime. Still, as with the blacks, Jews did play the game during the sport's formative period— and even as early as the 1850s and 1860s, when the Pike brothers, Boaz and Lipman, played baseball as amateurs in New York. Later, both of these gentlemen played with the famous Brooklyn Atlantics, and Lipman (or "Lip," as he was called) and still another brother, Jay, went on to become two of the very first professionals in the country.

But these were not the only nineteenth-century Jews in big-league baseball. There were others, such as "Chief" Jim Rosenman (outfielder for the Troy Nationals in 1882, and for various American Association clubs throughout the decade), Danny Stearns (who played every position but pitcher for several National League and American Association clubs in the eighties), Billy Nash (who for 15 years until the Spanish-American War played third base, mainly with the Boston and Philadelphia clubs of the National League, and who appeared in over 1,500 games during his career), and more, some of whom changed their obviously Jewish names to make it easier for them to play—for example, pitcher Harry Kane, whose true name was Harry Cohen.

And even in the very year 1910, when Regan and Stahl published their bigoted little joke, two of the greatest Jewish ballplayers of all time— "Big Ed" Reulbach (pitcher) and Johnny Kling (catcher)—were helping to bring the National League championship to Chicago for the fourth time in five years.

This "Jewish battery," on Frank Chance's renowned team of the decade, also happened to have performed the only feat of its kind in major-league history—specifically, "Big Ed" pitched, while Johnny Kling caught, both games of a doubleheader, and in doing so, registered two shutout triumphs in a row! The occasion was September 26, 1908; the opposing team was Brooklyn, and the scores were 5 to 0 and 3 to 0, with Reulbach giving up a total of only eight hits in both games. Furthermore, as *The New York Times* reported it, "Reulbach did not seem to be a bit tired."

As anti-Semitism waned in the major leagues, increasing numbers of Jewish athletes found their way into the sport; as with the breakdown of the racial barrier, so, too, the religious barrier disappeared.

The final irony is that all the "Moes," the "Solomons," and the "Skys" no longer need be concerned about changing their "cognomens" to play the game; their presence on the diamond has served only to enrich the pastime. Witness such names as Morris "Moe" Berg (he was a language scholar and a graduate of three universities), Charles Solomon Myer (he played in over 1,900 games and accumulated over 2,100 hits), Jacob "Jake" Pitler (he played second base for Pittsburgh and later was a coach for Brooklyn), Harry "The Horse" Danning (he covered home plate over a ten-year period with the Giants), Robert "Bo" Belinsky (he pitched a no-hit, no-run game against Baltimore in his very first season with Los Angeles), Art Shamsky (he helped the Mets win both the National League pennant and the World Series in 1969), Ron Blomberg (he captured the fans' affections in 1971, his rookie year with the Yankees, by pounding the ball for a season average of .322), "Hammerin' Hank" Greenberg (he was elected to baseball's Hall of Fame in 1956), and Sandy Koufax (he won three Cy Young Awards, among many others, and at the age of 36, became the youngest player ever elected to the Hall of Fame).

But if the story of the Jew and the black man in professional baseball has been one of struggle and achievement, in its own way—as has been shown—the story of the pastime itself also has been characterized by repeated triumphs over crises and conflicts. Indeed, even as late as 1914, when the fortunes of both the National and American Leagues seemed well assured, the specter of a new baseball struggle again darkened the nation's sports horizon. For as World War I flared on the battlefields of Europe, a group of American multimillionaire industrialists—James Gilmore (coal), Harry Sinclair (oil), the Ward baking family (bread and cake), Phillip Ball (ice), and others—invaded the territories of the two major leagues with a third professional circuit—the Federal League.

Employing the ancient lure of money—of which unlimited amounts were at their disposal—the Federals successfully tempted away dozens of outstanding players from National and American League clubs. Franchises were established in Brooklyn, Baltimore, Buffalo, Pittsburgh, Chicago, Kansas City, Indianapolis, and St. Louis; and for two years the Federal League conducted pennant races in direct competition with its rival circuits.

Then, as the United States headed for active participation in the European conflict, and as public interest in sports slackened, the realistic businessmen-backers of the new circuit suddenly decided to terminate their brief sortie into professional baseball. Agreements were reached with the National and American Leagues; the Federal League disbanded; and tranquillity once again returned to the national pastime.

The calm, however, proved to be the temporary lull before the traditional storm. For shortly thereafter, in 1920, the "Black Sox" scandal broke, the ramifications of which dismayed and disillusioned the American sports-minded public more than any previous such incident.

In a major effort to restore respectability to the pastime, the three-man National Commission was replaced by an Advisory Council dominated by a single supreme "Baseball Commissioner," who was given virtually unlimited powers to police the sport. Kenesaw Mountain Landis, the tough federal judge who once had fined the giant Standard Oil Company of Indiana the staggering sum of $29,240,000 for accepting rebates on freight, was the man chosen to hold the commissioner's post, and this he did until his death in 1944.

It was baseball's good fortune to be blessed at that critical moment of its history with the emergence of a new idol of the diamond, George Herman "Babe" Ruth; since more than any other single factor, it was the great Babe and his heroic feats at bat that dispelled the odious clouds of the Black Sox scandal.

Ruth both startled and impressed the baseball world in his very first year with the New York Yankees (1920), when he collected the grand total of fifty-four home runs for the season.*

* Ruth's batting feat coincided with the introduction into American League competition of the so-called "lively" or "rabbit" ball, which was stronger and harder than heretofore, consequently capable of being hit over greater distances.

The following year Ruth slammed out fifty-nine four-baggers; and finally, in 1927, the Bambino, as he was affectionately called, established the remarkable and durable record of sixty home runs hit in a single season. This total was exceeded in 1961 by Roger Maris, also of the Yankees, who hit sixty-one homers; but Maris's mark was made in a schedule of 162 games played, while Ruth's record was set during a 154-game season. Therefore, according to a ruling by Baseball Commissioner Frick, Ruth's record still stands.

Ruth played with the Yankees from 1920 to 1934. During that period, he became one of the most beloved of all baseball heroes, attracting over the years millions of paying fans to ballparks across the nation. The Babe amassed so many batting marks while with the Yankees that he became known as the "Sultan of Swat."

Some of the records established during his major-league career include the following: most home runs over a lifetime (714); most home runs in the American League (708); most home runs in World Series games (15); most runs batted in over a lifetime (2,209); most years hitting forty or more home runs (11); most years hitting fifty or more home runs (4); most bases received on balls over a lifetime (2,056); most total bases in a season (457), and so on.

So great has Ruth's reputation as a batter been that one of the more remarkable facts about the man has tended to become obscured—namely, that before his Yankee slugging days, Ruth was an outstanding pitcher for the Boston Red Sox. Indeed, during the World Series of 1916 and 1918, the Babe was undefeated in three out of three starts for the Sox. And in the process of achieving those three victories, he pitched a record total of 29 consecutive scoreless innings against Brooklyn and Chicago, respectively.

Comparisons often have been drawn between the accomplishments of George Herman Ruth and that other great ballplayer, Tyrus Cobb; but such discussions, at best, can be regarded only as idle speculation, for each man in his lifetime was a superb and popular athlete. In one strange and macabre respect, however, both shared a common destiny: Each was ultimately struck down and destroyed by the same disease, cancer.

In retrospect, it can be said that with the fortuitous appearance of Babe Ruth on the crisis-ridden scene of 1920, and with the establishment of the Office of the Commissioner of Baseball, the modern era had finally dawned. The American national pastime had survived its darkest moment of the twentieth century.

FOURTEEN

THE LUCK
OF
THE GAME

Our left fielder is sick and our catcher is lame;
Our short stop is playing a very poor game;
Two pitchers are used up, the other is wild;
The basemen can't play when the weather ain't mild;
The man in the right field is suffering from chills;
The "sub" has a strange complication of ills;
Just what bothers our captain the doctor can't tell—
But in other respects we are feeling quite well.

—Anonymous lament bemoaning
Chicago's hard luck in 1884.

An ancient tale told among the Cherokee Indians of North Carolina relates the story of a great ball game that once took place between the birds of the air and the four-footed animals of the earth. According to the legend, the contest was won by the birds, even though the land animals supposedly had the stronger team. And the victory was achieved solely by the additional margin of aid given to the birds by the lowly bat and the

tiny flying squirrel, whose assistance was refused by the four-footed creatures because of the insignificant size of its donors. For this reason, when
a Cherokee ballplayer prepares for a game, he usually invokes the good
will of the bat and the aid of the flying squirrel. And in addition, as a
further token of luck insurance, he frequently ties a small piece of bat-
wing to his ball stick or other game implement.

Baseball players, of course, do not go quite as far in preparing for
their contests, although it is known that many players do nurture pet
superstitions of their own to which they are bound almost as religiously.
Aside from cultivating the various conventional beliefs and superstitions
held by many persons—such as faith in magic charms, lucky coins, omens
and signs—ballplayers have been known to regard certain other phenomena, deeds, or occurrences as particularly forbidding or fortunate.

For example, some athletes believe that it is bad luck to go back and
fasten a missed buttonhole when dressing for a game. Others believe it
is equally unfortunate to meet a cross-eyed person on the day of a game
or to pass a funeral on the way to the ballpark.

On the other hand, good fortune on the ballfield is presaged for some
players by accidentally wearing an undershirt inside out beneath a
uniform; by seeing certain lucky numbers before a game; or, curiously,
by encountering a load of empty barrels on a wagon—a common sight
in the old beer garden-saloon days.

The great Ty Cobb, who it would seem needed nothing more than
his very presence to frighten an opposing pitcher, used to bear a big black
bat to every ball game after 1907. The oddity, however, was not the bat
—many players have favorite bats—but the fact that the mighty slugger
never used it; it was there just for luck.

The magic that Cobb ascribed to this particular piece of lumber was
that it was the bat he had wielded during the 1907 season, when he
topped the American League with an average of .350. In addition, it was
the bat he had held during the cake-cutting ceremony at his marriage,
also in 1907.

Bill "Buck" Ewing, who played with the New York Nationals from
1883 through 1892, also had a peculiar belief about bats. Ewing believed
that his hitting would be better if the club mascot would spit on his bat
before he went to the plate. How this helped him, of course, cannot be
determined, but Buck's lifetime batting average, covering 18 years, finally
came to .311.

On the other hand, Dick Buckley, Ewing's teammate on the Giants during 1890 and 1891, believed that a corroded old nail he owned was a source of luck, while Connie Mack, the venerable manager of the Athletics for half a century (1901–1950), relied on a dry old chestnut.

Carrying charms of one sort or another, in fact, has always been a common habit of ballplayers. "Orator" Jim O'Rourke, who covered the outfield for New York in the 1880s, for example, used to carry his latest batting average. Arthur "Bugs" Raymond, a former printer, used to carry his union card when pitching for the Giants and Cards early in the century. "Turkey Mike" Donlin, who aspired to the stage, and who was Raymond's teammate on the Giants in 1911, used to carry a tattered theater program. While George "Rube" Waddell, the great pitching star of the early Philadelphia and St. Louis Americans, used to carry a delicate little watch hand.

Waddell, incidentally, even got his nickname through a "lucky"— or "unlucky"—accident, as the case may be. Rube himself told the story back in 1903:

> I got my nickname of "Rube" in Franklin, Pa., in 1896, the first year I played professional ball. I had pitched a morning game at Oil City and shut the team out 8 to 0. In the afternoon both teams returned to Franklin for another game. The man intending to pitch for us got drunk, so I went in again. In the second inning, with the score 2 to 0 against us, a line ball hit me in the forehead and knocked me unconscious for about five minutes. I was sore and insisted on pitching out the game. We beat them 16 to 2, and they did not get another man to first base, while I made two home runs, two double-baggers and a single. That night the manager of the Oil City met me on the street and said: "You're a regular robber; no one but a 'rube' could recover from an accident like that and finish the game." That fastened the nickname to me and it has stuck.

One of the oddest talismans of all was that belonging to Harry "Judge" Lumley, who played the outfield for Brooklyn from 1904 until 1910. "Judge" Lumley used to carry for luck a small strand of the cable used in building the Brooklyn Bridge, which was begun in 1870 and completed in 1883.

But if some ballplayers carried charms, others wore them. For example, George "Piano Legs" Gore, the veteran outfielder of the Chicago and New York Nationals (1880s and 1890s), always wore a pair of "lucky yellow" garters on the diamond. "Big Ed" Reulbach, one of Chicago's early hurlers, wore a special "winning" cap when pitching. Roger Connor, the Irish first baseman of the nineteenth-century Giants and St. Louis Nationals, wore a lucky shamrock. While Weston Fisler, who played first base for the Philadelphia Athletics in the 1870s, wore a small paper collar fastened around his neck. The collar served not only as an amulet but also as an indication of how cool a player Weston was. For when the game was over, Fisler, who was also called "the icicle," would ceremoniously remove the collar to demonstrate to all and sundry that it was just as fresh as when he first had put it on.

There is a case on record in which the player's luck changed so radically that if one were not truly superstitious, he would abandon charms completely. The case involved Eddie "Vic" Cicotte, the reliable pitcher of the early Red Sox, and later the White Sox, who used to wear a strand of red ribbon around his left ankle for luck. But despite whatever prior fortune the red ribbon had brought Cicotte, all his luck ran out in 1920 when he was caught up in the infamous "Black Sox" scandal and was banned from the sport for life.

As indicated earlier, not all baseball superstitions involve carrying or wearing charms; there are also beliefs, rituals, habits, or actions. For example, a common belief is that if a player should trip en route to the field, he must, for "insurance," reverse his steps and carefully walk over the stumbling block. Also, if a pitcher should snap a shoelace during a game, instead of replacing the old lace with a new one, he must, for luck, tie the broken ends together and continue to pitch. In fact, way back in May 1884, Adrian Anson gave a Chicago newspaper correspondent the following facetious reason for his team's poor showing:

> We have been handicapped by our inability to secure the quality of shoestrings to which we have been accustomed for the past five years. The Eastern clubs, knowing how largely we have depended upon this peculiar brand of lacing, formed a pool and purchased all the shoestrings of that manufacture in the market. Such action was unfair and unprofessional, and it completely unnerved every member of the team.

The famous trio of Chicago—Tinker, Evers, and Chance—also had their peculiarities with regard to fortune on the field. For example, Joe Tinker, the shortstop, had the ritual habit of always walking directly to the plate on his first time up. If he got on base, he would on his next

ROGER CONNOR
Slugging first baseman for New York, 1883-1894
Hit .371 in 1885, .354 in 1886, and .382 in 1887.

WESTON D. FISLER
A cool first baseman.
He was called "the icicle."

appearance again use the direct approach. However, if he was put out, to break the jinx, he would first circle the plate before taking his second turn at bat.

Johnny Evers, the second baseman, believed in "saving" his luck. That is, if he was hitting well in practice, he would suddenly stop hitting the ball and retire to the bench to "save" his batting for the game.

Frank Chance, the third member of the trio, used to wander around his first-base sack before a game, seeking lucky four-leaf clovers.

Chance, by the way, who was also the club manager, once refused to allow his team to be photographed before the end of the season. He believed it might jinx the players. As events turned out, Chicago won the pennant that year (1908) on the basis of its victory over the Giants in the famous "Merkle" playoff, after which the team took on Detroit in the World Series and won, four games to one.

Still other superstitions involve little-noticed actions taken on the playing field itself, such as a player always placing his glove in a certain spot and moving it to another if the team is losing, or a player spitting a certain "magical" way before going to bat.

Lou Browning, the old Midwestern outfielder of the eighties and nineties, used to habitually come in from the field via third base, and in the process, would carefully step over the sack without touching it. "Old Fox" Griffith, on the other hand, who pitched for Chicago in the nineties, would enter the box only after he had clapped his hands a certain number of times.

There was even a time when baseball teams themselves were regarded as omens of good fortune. For example, in April of 1891, Henry Chadwick wrote the following:

> I am reminded of a remark I heard made on Friday morning last week by a lady as she was being assisted on the train by her escort at the Grand Central Depot. She said: "How about that tunnel, Harry, I feel awfully nervous?" "Oh," he remarked, "you need not fear a bit; we have a baseball team on the train." It has come to be that a ball team on board a train amounts to a sort of mascotte for a safe journey, so seldom have serious accidents occurred to baseball travelers.

With regard to travel, that, too, carried mysterious implications to certain players. Frank Chance, for one, who has already been mentioned as having been a most superstitious individual, would not sleep on a train unless he did so in lower-berth 13. If no such accommodation was available, Chance would sleep in the stateroom, but only after scribbling the number 13 on the door outside.

Indeed, numbers have always had special significance to ballplayers. The numbers 3, 4, 5, and 7, for instance, no longer may be worn on the uniforms of any member of the New York Yankees. Those numbers are "retired," for they once belonged to four of baseball's greatest stars: number 3 to Babe Ruth, number 4 to Lou Gehrig, number 5 to Joe DiMaggio, and number 7 to Mickey Mantle.

But whether a player wears a certain number or not, or is superstitious or not, most people will agree that the best stock in trade (or magic) on which an athlete can rely is his own native ability, playing skill, and physical condition, coupled with a wholesome spirit and determination to win.

Native ability, of course, is something one has or has not, in varying degrees or amounts. But the other attributes, all of which are desirable, if not essential, can be either developed or improved.

In ancient Greece, athletes often improved their physical condition by rigidly restricting their diets. Some did not eat meat of any kind but lived mainly on dried figs, cheese, and wheat. Others, by contrast, ate great quantities of beef and pork; while still others lived largely on goat flesh.

Roman athletes, on the other hand, kept in shape by not drinking liquids for long periods, holding themselves in prolonged states of thirst. Also, many Romans-in-training consumed mighty portions of half-cooked, half-raw meat.

But perhaps the most fascinating preparation for a ball game—and the one involving the closest approach to superstition and magic—was the pregame ritual of the Cherokee ballplayer. James Mooney, writing in *The American Anthropologist* during the latter part of the last century, described it as follows:

> The player renders himself an object of terror to his opponent by eating a rattlesnake which has been killed and cooked by the shaman [Indian high priest]. He rubs himself with an eelskin to make himself slippery like the eel, and rubs each limb down once with the fore and hind leg of a turtle, because the legs of that animal are remarkably stout. He applies to the shaman to conjure a dangerous opponent so that he may be unable to see the ball in its flight, or may dislocate a wrist or break a leg. Sometimes the shaman draws upon the ground an armless figure of his rival with a hole where the heart should be. Into this hole he drops two black beads, covers them with earth, and stamps upon them, and thus the dreaded rival is doomed.

It is hardly conceivable that before a game an anxious baseball player would eat a rattlesnake for luck or, for that matter, go through any of the other rites described. Yet, at one time in the history of the sport, some big-league pitchers were "spiritually," if not literally, linked with snakes.

In the 1870s, for example, pitchers were beginning to discover that they could do various odd things with the ball—make it hop, drop, shoot inward, outward, sink, etc. But for many years, both the public and baseball players alike could not quite believe what they thought they saw the ball do. And on various occasions, special pitching exhibitions were even staged to demonstrate whether a baseball actually could be made to curve or react in some other controlled manner during flight.

By 1881, public skepticism had reached such proportions that when two pitchers of the Chicago Nationals—Lawrence Corcoran and Fred Goldsmith—developed a couple of good curve balls, this is what the *Buffalo Courier* said: "Goldsmith and Corcoran are pitching 'snake' balls. We wonder how much whisky a man must carry to be a good 'snake' pitcher?"

And the *Troy Times*, commenting in a similar vein about its own home team, observed: "It is something besides the Chicago pitcher that makes the Troy Club 'see snakes' so often."

Indeed, public doubt about the veracity of curve pitching remained so strong that Edward J. Prindle, in a booklet called "The Art of Zigzag Curve Pitching," written about 1890 and published in 1895, was careful to include an almost apologetic and pleading preface to the work. This is what Prindle said:

> I am well aware that the subject discussed in the following pages is one of extreme delicacy and intricacy and for that reason I very much doubt if this work meets with a universally favorable reception. In using the word "favorable" I do not intend to use it as applying to a large sale but to the acceptation of the truth of the hypothesis involved . . . It requires considerable nerve to appear thus boldly on untrodden ground, for, so far as I am aware, the subject is here handled for the first time. For that reason be as charitable as you can and be not too hasty to condemn my work.

Of course, since Prindle's time, it has been repeatedly demonstrated, and publicly accepted, that a pitcher with speed and control can make a baseball behave in a remarkable variety of unexpected ways while the ball is traveling to the plate.

The first professional pitcher to have developed the knack of curving a ball in flight is reputed to have been William Arthur Cummings, of the old Mutual Base Ball Club. This is generally acknowledged and is further supported by a letter to the editor of *The New York Times*, written apropos curve pitching in the summer of 1900 by James Gordon Spencer, one of Cummings' early teammates:

I have always claimed that Arthur Cummings was the original curve pitcher. Some time between 1863 and 1870 I belonged to the Carroll Baseball Club, which played in a field back of Carroll Park, in Brooklyn, and Cummings, just from school, was our pitcher. The Star Baseball Club played on the same grounds, and took Cummings for their pitcher because he pitched a "curve," which it was hard to hit. After playing for a time with the Stars Cummings was put on the Mutuals, and afterward, I think, was for a time with the Providence club.

I am positive that Cummings pitched with a curve before 1870, and I think as early as 1864. The curve was natural to him, and I do not think was the result of study, but was none the less acknowledged and effective.

—James Gordon Spencer.
Honolulu, H.I., July 4, 1900.

The first pitcher among the amateurs, on the other hand, to have hurled a curve ball is said to have been Joseph M. Mann, of the Princeton University team, who unleashed his curve in a game against Yale, back in 1875.

Appropriately, it was also in 1875 that the first catcher's mitt was used. What with "snake" balls and all being thrown, catchers needed more than just luck to endure the severe pounding their hands received.

William "Gunner" McGunnigle, who caught for the Fall River team, and later pitched for Buffalo and Worcester, is credited with being the first to employ some form of protection behind the plate. As the baseball guide for 1895 relates it:

> . . . his hands became very sore, and to protect them he purchased a pair of bricklayers' gloves, cut the fingers off and used them in a game against the Harvard nine. Tyng, who was catching for the Harvards, took up the idea at once. Buck Ewing was the first catcher to use the "pillow" glove for the left hand, and had to endure a good deal of "chaffing" for a long time. Catcher Tyng afterwards invented the catcher's mask.

Actually, the mask was invented before that, in 1873, by Fred W. Thayer, who modeled it after a fencing mask with the wire mesh slit open to provide greater visibility. James Tyng, however, was the first catcher to regularly employ the mask in college games; and by 1877, the protective "cage" had come into general professional use.

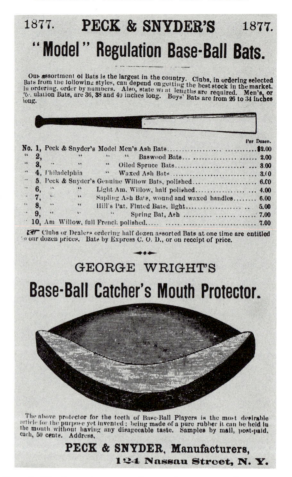

Baseball advertisement featuring a mouth protector
for the teeth of baseball players, 1877.

With the growing acceptance of masks and gloves, a special catcher's superstition arose, especially in connection with the oversized mitt. Specifically, it was regarded as bad luck for any player other than the catcher to wear it. A player could borrow the catcher's ordinary practice glove without jeopardy, but beware the jinx if he happened to slip his paw into the "big mitt," as it was called.

Chest protectors for catchers made their appearance in 1885, but it was not until the first decade of the twentieth century that Charles "Red" Dooin of the Philadelphia Nationals and Roger "Duke" Bresnahan of the

New York Nationals introduced shinguards to protect a catcher's legs.

Bresnahan, incidentally, sought "protection" on the diamond in still another way. In addition to his regular gear, he concealed a badge inside his uniform. For, interestingly, the Duke earned his living between seasons as a detective.

However, lest the impression be conveyed that all was mayhem for the man behind the plate in the nineteenth century, let it be said that in the early days the catcher did not stand directly behind the batter, but a considerable distance farther back, where he was able to catch the ball after it had already bounced. It was not until the turn of the century that catchers moved up close behind the plate; even so, many old-time, bare-handed, unmasked, and otherwise unprotected catchers suffered severe injuries from foul tips and swiftly pitched balls. Those men truly needed all the luck they could get, and from whatever source.

One of the first catchers—if not the very first—to play directly behind the plate was the dauntless Nathaniel Woodhull Hicks, who caught in the 1870s for the old Mutual baseball team of the National Association. Hicks obviously was capable of absorbing terrific physical punishment, for despite numerous injuries sustained while playing "up close," without protection, he nevertheless continued to play the game in the spot he believed to be most effective for the position he covered—directly behind the batter.

An early account describes old Nat's performance in a game against the Atlantics as follows:

> In consequence of the severe injuries already received by Hicks, it was not thought by any that he could play at all, or if he attempted to play in his crippled condition he would certainly make a bungle of it. But in this they were greatly mistaken, for, far from losing the game, he actually won it by his brilliant play . . . He went into the game with his right eye almost knocked out of his head and his nose and the whole right side of his face swollen to three times their normal size. Yet, notwithstanding this, nothing seemed too difficult for him to take. Player after player went down before his unfaltering nerve, and although struck four times during the game—once squarely on the mouth by the ball and once on the chest and twice with the bat—he could not be driven away from his position. Indeed, taking it all in all, no man ever exhibited more nerve and pluck combined with cool, calculating judgment than did this man and he certainly deserved all the applause and commendation that he received.

Other catchers who were in Hicks's class at the time and performed similar feats were "Fergie" Malone, "Mart" King, and "Doug" Allison.

During the season, Malone commonly went about with blackened eyes and bruised, swollen cheeks, so regularly was he struck in the face by foul balls. King's calloused hands could best be described as looking like twin hams, his fingers were so misshapen by catching injuries; while Allison's features were so battered out of shape that he closely resembled a punch-drunk fighter.

It is to men like these, with their skill, daring, and determination to play despite the danger, that credit must be given for helping to bring down the high scores that marked so many early games.

Three and a half centuries have passed since the Pilgrims arrived in this hemisphere and first played ball in the New World. The intervening years have witnessed the growth of America and the shrinking of the planet. The time between has been far from uneventful—indeed, the centuries have been filled with periods of struggle, expansion, strife and tranquillity. Yet, through it all, a mighty nation has emerged, and today man stands on the threshold of another "New World"—the realm of outer space and the stars.

In a parallel way, the American national pastime has grown from a primitive game to a sophisticated sport. Baseball has had its years of struggle and change, its periods of strife and hardship, and its days of glory. The years ahead undoubtedly will bring additional unpredictable changes, greater excitement, and more pleasure to untold millions of fans. Nevertheless, the debt to the past must be acknowledged and honored, for the sparkling brilliance that characterizes baseball today is only the distant reflection of the historic diamond in the rough.

INDEX

ILLUSTRATION CREDITS

Courtesy The New-York Historical Society: pages 38, 81, 108, 109, 143, 188, 199

Courtesy General Research and Humanities Division, The New York Public Library, Astor, Lenox and Tilden Foundations: pages 11, 22, 23, 24, 25, 29, 31, 39, 40, 41, 43, 50, 51, 56, 57, 58, 60, 62, 63, 69, 72, 73, 76, 78, 79, 82, 84, 85, 86, 90, 91, 93, 94, 95, 96, 99, 104, 106, 107, 110, 111, 112, 113, 114, 115, 118, 119, 121, 126, 129, 140, 142, 146, 150, 151, 152, 154, 157, 158, 159, 163, 164, 166, 167, 168, 169, 170, 171, 172, 173, 174, 183, 189 191, 195, 197, 201, 202, 203, 213, 218

Courtesy U. S. Postal Service: page 198